TASK CARD SERIES

Conceived and written by
Ron Marson
Illustrated by
Peg Marson

TOPS LEARNING SYSTEMS

10970 S. Mulino Rd.
Canby OR 97013

Oh, those pesky COPYRIGHT RESTRICTIONS!

Dear Educator,

TOPS is a nonprofit organization dedicated to educational ideals, not our bottom line. We have invested much time, energy, money, and love to bring you this excellent teaching resource.

And we have carefully designed this book to run on simple materials you already have or can easily purchase. If you consider the depth and quality of this curriculum amortized over years of teaching, it is dirt cheap, orders of magnitude less than prepackaged kits and textbooks.

Please honor our copyright restrictions. We are a very small company, and book sales are our life blood. When you buy this book and use it for your own teaching, you sustain our publishing effort. If you give or "loan" this book or copies of our lessons to other teachers, with no compensation to TOPS, you squeeze us financially, and may drive us out of business. Our well-being rests in your hands.

What if you are excited about the terrific ideas in this book, and want to share them with your colleagues? What if the teacher down the hall, or your homeschooling neighbor, is begging you for good science, quick! We have suggestions. Please see our *Purchase and Royalty Options* below.

We are grateful for the work you are doing to help shape tomorrow. We are honored that you are making TOPS a part of your teaching effort. Thank you for your good will and kind support.

Sincerely, Ron Marson

Purchase and Royalty Options:

Individual teachers, homeschoolers, libraries:

PURCHASE option: If your colleagues ask to borrow your book, please ask them to read this copyright page, and to contact TOPS for our current catalog so they can purchase their own book. We also have an **online catalog** that you can access at www.topscience.org.

If you are reselling a **used book** to another classroom teacher or homeschooler, please be aware that this still affects us by eliminating a potential book sale. We do not push "newer and better" editions to encourage consumerism. So we ask seller or purchaser (or both!) to acknowledge the ongoing value of this book by sending a contribution to support our continued work. Let your conscience be your guide.

Honor System ROYALTIES: If you wish to make copies from a library, or pass on copies of just a few activities in this book, please calculate their value at 50 cents (25 cents for homeschoolers) per lesson per recipient. Send that amount, or ask the recipient to send that amount, to TOPS. We also gladly accept donations. We know life is busy, but please do follow through on your good intentions promptly. It will only take a few minutes, and you'll know you did the right thing!

Schools and Districts:

You may wish to use this curriculum in several classrooms, in one or more schools. Please observe the following:

PURCHASE option: Order this book in quantities equal to the number of target classrooms. If you order 5 books, for example, then you have unrestricted use of this curriculum in any 5 classrooms per year for the life of your institution. You may order at these quantity discounts:

2-9 copies: 90% of current catalog price + shipping.

10+ copies: 80% of current catalog price + shipping.

ROYALTY option: Purchase 1 book *plus* photocopy or printing rights in quantities equal to the number of designated classrooms. If you pay for 5 Class Licenses, for example, then you have purchased reproduction rights for any 5 classrooms per year for the life of your institution.

1-9 Class Licenses: 70% of current book price per classroom.

10+ Class Licenses: 60% of current book price per classroom.

Workshops and Training Programs:

We are grateful to all of you who spread the word about TOPS. Please limit duplication to only those lessons you will be using, and collect all copies afterward. No take-home copies, please. Copies of copies are prohibited. Ask us for a free shipment of as many current **TOPS Ideas** catalogs as you need to support your efforts. Every catalog contains numerous free sample teaching ideas.

Current edition printed 2001

Copyright © 1992 by TOPS Learning Systems. All rights reserved. Printed in the United States of America. No part of this book may be used or reproduced in any manner whatsoever without written permission from the publisher, except as explicitly stated below:

The individual OWNER of this book has our permission to make multiple copies of any student materials for PERSONAL classroom or homeschool use, provided such reproductions bear copyright notice. Reproduction of student materials from libraries is permitted if the user compensates TOPS as outlined above. Reproduction of these pages by schools, school systems or teacher training programs for wider dissemination, or by anyone for commercial sale, is strictly prohibited unless licensing for such has been purchased from **TOPS Learning Systems, 10970 S Mulino Rd, Canby OR 97013.**

ISBN 0-941008-86-X

CONTENTS

PART I — INTRODUCTION

A. A TOPS Model for Effective Science Teaching
C. Getting Ready
D. Gathering Materials
E. Sequencing Task Cards
F. Long Range Objectives
G. Review / Test Questions

PART II — TEACHING NOTES

CORE CURRICULUM
1. Squeeze Play
2. Pressure Print
3. Pascal's Principle
4. Press your Advantage
5. Ocean of Air
6. Snap and Pop
7. Towers of Water
8. Rise and Fall (1)
9. Breathing Machine
10. Bubbles Up
11. A Closed System
12. Submarine
13. Build a Manometer
14. Centimeters of Water
15. U Tube / Straight Tube
16. Rise and Fall (2)
17. Rise and Fall (3)
18. Inflow / Outflow
19. Bernoulli's Principle
20. Atomizers
21. Airfoil
22. Spin and Curve

ENRICHMENT CURRICULUM
23. Steam to Stream
24. A Perfect Vacuum?
25. A Very Tall Test Tube
26. Measure the Pressure
27. Vacuum Pump
28. Battery Pressure
29. Maximum Lung Pressure
30. Big Lift
31. Three Variables
32. Aneroid Barometer

PART III — REPRODUCIBLE STUDENT TASK CARDS

Task Cards 1-32
Supplementary Pages – centimeter grid
  area estimator: square inches
  area estimator: square centimeters
  centimeter ruler
  pressure scale

A TOPS Model for Effective Science Teaching...

If science were only a set of explanations and a collection of facts, you could teach it with blackboard and chalk. You could assign students to read chapters and answer the questions that followed. Good students would take notes, read the text, turn in assignments, then give you all this information back again on a final exam. Science is traditionally taught in this manner. Everybody learns the same body of information at the same time. Class togetherness is preserved.

But science is more than this.

Science is also process — a dynamic interaction of rational inquiry and creative play. Scientists probe, poke, handle, observe, question, think up theories, test ideas, jump to conclusions, make mistakes, revise, synthesize, communicate, disagree and discover. Students can understand science as process only if they are free to think and act like scientists, in a classroom that recognizes and honors individual differences.

Science is *both* a traditional body of knowledge *and* an individualized process of creative inquiry. Science as process cannot ignore tradition. We stand on the shoulders of those who have gone before. If each generation reinvents the wheel, there is no time to discover the stars. Nor can traditional science continue to evolve and redefine itself without process. Science without this cutting edge of discovery is a static, dead thing.

Here is a teaching model that combines the best of both elements into one integrated whole. It is only a model. Like any scientific theory, it must give way over time to new and better ideas. We challenge you to incorporate this TOPS model into your own teaching practice. Change it and make it better so it works for you.

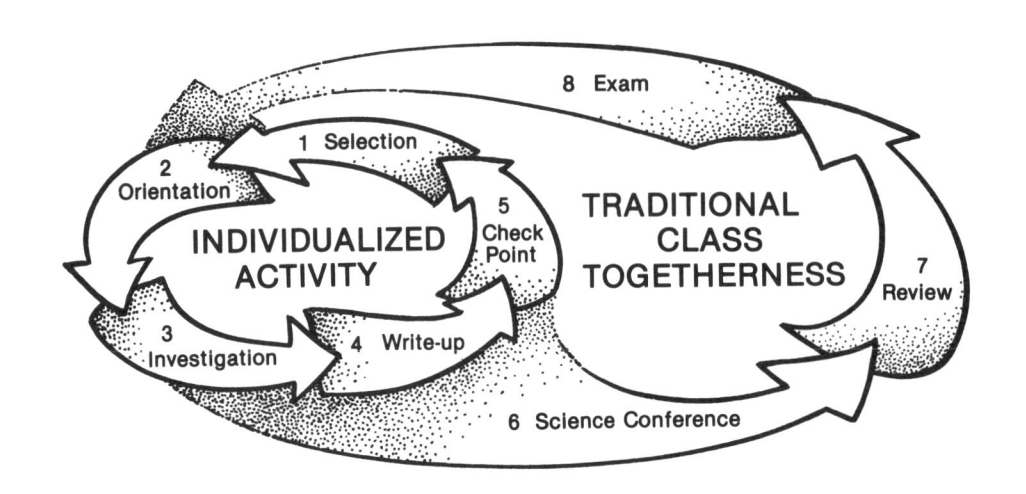

1. SELECTION

Doing TOPS is as easy as selecting the first task card and doing what it says, then the second, then the third, and so on. Working at their own pace, students fall into a natural routine that creates stability and order. They still have questions and problems, to be sure, but students know where they are and where they need to go.

Students generally select task cards in sequence because new concepts build on old ones in a specific order. There are, however, exceptions to this rule: students might *skip* a task that is not challenging; *repeat* a task with doubtful results; *add* a task of their own design to answer original "what would happen if" questions.

2. ORIENTATION

Many students will simply read a task card and immediately understand what to do. Others will require further verbal interpretation. Identify poor readers in your class. When they ask, "What does this mean?" they may be asking in reality, "Will you please read this card aloud?"

With such a diverse range of talent among students, how can you individualize activity and still hope to finish this module as a cohesive group? It's easy. By the time your most advanced students have completed all the task cards, including the enrichment series at the end, your slower students have at least completed the basic core curriculum. This core provides the common background so necessary for meaningful discussion, review and testing on a class basis.

3. INVESTIGATION

Students work through the task cards independently and cooperatively. They follow their own experimental strategies and help each other. You encourage this behavior by helping students only *after* they have tried to help themselves. As a resource person, you work to stay *out* of the center of attention, answering student questions rather than posing teacher questions.

When you need to speak to everyone at once, it is appropriate to interrupt individual task card activity and address the whole class, rather than repeat yourself over and over again. If you plan ahead, you'll find that most interruptions can fit into brief introductory remarks at the beginning of each new period.

4. WRITE-UP

Task cards ask students to explain the "how and why" of things. Write-ups are brief and to the point. Students may accelerate their pace through the task cards by writing these reports out of class.

Students may work alone or in cooperative lab groups. But each one must prepare an original write-up. These must be brought to the teacher for approval as soon as they are completed. Avoid dealing with too many write-ups near the end of the module, by enforcing this simple rule: each write-up must be approved *before* continuing on to the next task card.

5. CHECK POINT

The student and teacher evaluate each write-up together on a pass/no pass basis. (Thus no time is wasted haggling over grades.) If the student has made reasonable effort consistent with individual ability, the write-up is checked off on a progress chart and included in the student's personal assignment folder or notebook kept on file in class.

Because the student is present when you evaluate, feedback is immediate and effective. A few seconds of this direct student-teacher interaction is surely more effective than 5 minutes worth of margin notes that students may or may not heed. Remember, you don't have to point out every error. Zero in on particulars. If reasonable effort has not been made, direct students to make specific improvements, and see you again for a follow-up check point.

A responsible lab assistant can double the amount of individual attention each student receives. If he or she is mature and respected by your students, have the assistant check the even-numbered write-ups while you check the odd ones. This will balance the work load and insure that all students receive equal treatment.

6. SCIENCE CONFERENCE

After individualized task card activity has ended, this is a time for students to come together, to discuss experimental results, to debate and draw conclusions. Slower students learn about the enrichment activities of faster students. Those who did original investigations, or made unusual discoveries, share this information with their peers, just like scientists at a real conference. This conference is open to films, newspaper articles and community speakers. It is a perfect time to consider the technological and social implications of the topic you are studying.

7. READ AND REVIEW

Does your school have an adopted science textbook? Do parts of your science syllabus still need to be covered? Now is the time to integrate other traditional science resources into your overall program. Your students already share a common background of hands-on lab work. With this shared base of experience, they can now read the text with greater understanding, think and problem-solve more successfully, communicate more effectively.

You might spend just a day on this step or an entire week. Finish with a review of key concepts in preparation for the final exam. Test questions in this module provide an excellent basis for discussion and study.

8. EXAM

Use any combination of the review/test questions, plus questions of your own, to determine how well students have mastered the concepts they've been learning. Those who finish your exam early might begin work on the first activity in the next new TOPS module.

Now that your class has completed a major TOPS learning cycle, it's time to start fresh with a brand new topic. Those who messed up and got behind don't need to stay there. Everyone begins the new topic on an equal footing. This frequent change of pace encourages your students to work hard, to enjoy what they learn, and thereby grow in scientific literacy.

GETTING READY

Here is a checklist of things to think about and preparations to make before your first lesson.

☐ Decide if this TOPS module is the best one to teach next.

TOPS modules are flexible. They can generally be scheduled in any order to meet your own class needs. Some lessons within certain modules, however, do require basic math skills or a knowledge of fundamental laboratory techniques. Review the task cards in this module now if you are not yet familiar with them. Decide whether you should teach any of these other TOPS modules first: *Measuring Length, Graphing, Metric Measure, Weighing* or *Electricity* (before *Magnetism*). It may be that your students already possess these requisite skills or that you can compensate with extra class discussion or special assistance.

☐ Number your task card masters in pencil.

The small number printed in the lower right corner of each task card shows its position within the overall series. If this ordering fits your schedule, copy each number into the blank parentheses directly above it at the top of the card. Be sure to use pencil rather than ink. You may decide to revise, upgrade or rearrange these task cards next time you teach this module. To do this, write your own better ideas on blank 4 x 6 index cards, and renumber them into the task card sequence wherever they fit best. In this manner, your curriculum will adapt and grow as you do.

☐ Copy your task card masters.

You have our permission to reproduce these task cards, for as long as you teach, with only 1 restriction: please limit the distribution of copies you make to the students you personally teach. Encourage other teachers who want to use this module to purchase their *own* copy. This supports TOPS financially, enabling us to continue publishing new TOPS modules for you. For a full list of task card options, please turn to the first task card masters numbered "cards 1-2."

☐ Collect needed materials.

Please see the opposite page.

☐ Organize a way to track completed assignment.

Keep write-ups on file in class. If you lack a vertical file, a box with a brick will serve. File folders or notebooks both make suitable assignment organizers. Students will feel a sense of accomplishment as they see their file folders grow heavy, or their notebooks fill up, with completed assignments. Easy reference and convenient review are assured, since all papers remain in one place.

Ask students to staple a sheet of numbered graph paper to the inside front cover of their file folder or notebook. Use this paper to track each student's progress through the module. Simply initial the corresponding task card number as students turn in each assignment.

☐ Review safety procedures.

Most TOPS experiments are safe even for small children. Certain lessons, however, require heat from a candle flame or Bunsen burner. Others require students to handle sharp objects like scissors, straight pins and razor blades. These task cards should not be attempted by immature students unless they are closely supervised. You might choose instead to turn these experiments into teacher demonstrations.

Unusual hazards are noted in the teaching notes and task cards where appropriate. But the curriculum cannot anticipate irresponsible behavior or negligence. It is ultimately the teacher's responsibility to see that common sense safety rules are followed at all times. Begin with these basic safety rules:

1. Eye Protection: Wear safety goggles when heating liquids or solids to high temperatures.
2. Poisons: Never taste anything unless told to do so.
3. Fire: Keep loose hair or clothing away from flames. Point test tubes which are heating away from your face and your neighbor's.
4. Glass Tubing: Don't force through stoppers. (The teacher should fit glass tubes to stoppers in advance, using a lubricant.)
5. Gas: Light the match first, before turning on the gas.

☐ Communicate your grading expectations.

Whatever your philosophy of grading, your students need to understand the standards you expect and how they will be assessed. Here is a grading scheme that counts individual effort, attitude and overall achievement. We think these 3 components deserve equal weight:

1. Pace (effort): Tally the number of check points you have initialed on the graph paper attached to each student's file folder or science notebook. Low ability students should be able to keep pace with gifted students, since write-ups are evaluated relative to individual performance standards. Students with absences or those who tend to work at a slow pace may (or may not) choose to overcome this disadvantage by assigning themselves more homework out of class.

2. Participation (attitude): This is a subjective grade assigned to reflect each student's attitude and class behavior. Active participators who work to capacity receive high marks. Inactive onlookers, who waste time in class and copy the results of others, receive low marks.

3. Exam (achievement): Task cards point toward generalizations that provide a base for hypothesizing and predicting. A final test over the entire module determines whether students understand relevant theory and can apply it in a predictive way.

Gathering Materials

Listed below is everything you'll need to teach this module. You already have many of these items. The rest are available from your supermarket, drugstore and hardware store. Laboratory supplies may be ordered through a science supply catalog. Hobby stores also carry basic science equipment.

Keep this classification key in mind as you review what's needed:

special in-a-box materials:	general on-the-shelf materials:
Italic type suggests that these materials are unusual. Keep these specialty items in a separate box. After you finish teaching this module, label the box for storage and put it away, ready to use again the next time you teach this module.	Normal type suggests that these materials are common. Keep these basics on shelves or in drawers that are readily accessible to your students. The next TOPS module you teach will likely utilize many of these same materials.
(substituted materials):	*optional materials:
Parentheses enclosing any item suggests a ready substitute. These alternatives may work just as well as the original, perhaps better. Don't be afraid to improvise, to make do with what you have.	An asterisk sets these items apart. They are nice to have, but you can easily live without them. They are probably not worth the extra trip, unless you are gathering other materials as well.

Everything is listed in order of first use. Start gathering at the top of this list and work down. Ask students to bring recycled items from home. The teaching notes may occasionally suggest additional student activity under the heading "Extensions." Materials for these optional experiments are listed neither here nor in the teaching notes. Read the extension itself to find out what new materials, if any, are required.

Needed quantities depend on how many students you have, how you organize them into activity groups, and how you teach. Decide which of these 3 estimates best applies to you, then adjust quantities up or down as necessary:

$Q_1 / Q_2 / Q_3$
- **Single Student:** Enough for 1 student to do all the experiments.
- **Individualized Approach:** Enough for 30 students informally working in 10 lab groups, all self-paced.
- **Traditional Approach:** Enough for 30 students, organized into 10 lab groups, all doing the same lesson.

KEY:	*special in-a-box materials*	general on-the-shelf materials
	(substituted materials)	*optional materials

1/1/1	*cup oil-based modeling clay*	
1/10/10	index cards	
1/10/10	pair of scissors	
1/2/4	*bathroom scales	
1/10/10	*calculators	
1/5/5	rolls masking tape	
5/50/50	*straight plastic straws – 1/4 inch diameter or slightly less*	
2/20/20	*meters 1/4 inch diameter tubing – see notes 3*	
3/30/30	plastic sandwich bags	
4/40/40	*meters string*	
3/9/30	textbooks	
2/20/20	*plastic produce bags*	
1/10/10	paper clips	
3/30/30	*canning jars with lids and rings that fit – see notes 5*	
1/6/10	*small plastic syringes, about 3 cc*	
1/4/10	*large plastic syringes, about 30 cc*	
1/10/10	small test tubes	
1/10/10	large test tubes	
1/10/10	plastic dishpans – see notes 7	
1/1/1	source of water – see notes 7	
1/10/10	baby food jars (beakers)	
1/10/10	*clear soft-plastic drinking cups – see notes 8*	
1/6/10	large nails, about 8 cm long	
1/6/10	needle-nose pliers – see notes 8	
6/60/60	*washers to fit 1/4 inch bolts – see notes 8*	
1/10/10	small balloons	
3/30/30	large rubber bands	
2/20/20	eyedroppers	
2/20/20	*wooden matches*	
1/10/10	cereal boxes	
2/20/20	cups sand (gravel or dirt)	
1/1/1	bottle food coloring	
1/1/1	*jar petroleum jelly*	
1/10/10	clothespins	
1/4/10	pie tins	
1/6/10	medium-sized tin cans	
1/4/10	funnels – long stem is best	
2/20/20	paper towels	
1/6/10	Ping-Pong balls	
1/6/10	*cardboard toilet tissue tubes*	
1/2/5	paper punches	
1/6/10	candles and matches	
1/10/10	graduated cylinders – 100 ml	
1/4/10	*large plastic milk jugs*	
2/20/20	*BB shot pellets*	
2/20/20	size-D batteries, dead or alive	
1/4/10	*gram balances	
1/4/10	long clipboards (*plywood squares*, thick telephone books)	
1/1/1	*bottle rubbing alcohol*	
1/4/10	film canisters (pill containers)	
1/1/1	roll plastic wrap	
1/4/10	*flat toothpicks	
1/10/10	*large cider jugs*	

D

Sequencing Task Cards

This logic tree shows how all the task cards in this module tie together. In general, students begin at the trunk of the tree and work up through the related branches. As the diagram suggests, the way to upper level activities leads up from lower level activities.

At the teacher's discretion, certain activities can be omitted or sequences changed to meet specific class needs. The only activities that must be completed in sequence are indicated by leaves that open *vertically* into the ones above them. In these cases the lower activity is a prerequisite to the upper.

When possible, students should complete the task cards in the same sequence as numbered. If time is short, however, or certain students need to catch up, you can use the logic tree to identify concept-related *horizontal* activities. Some of these might be omitted since they serve only to reinforce learned concepts rather than introduce new ones.

On the other hand, if students complete all the activities at a certain horizontal concept level, then experience difficulty at the next higher level, you might go back down the logic tree to have students repeat specific key activities for greater reinforcement.

For whatever reason, when you wish to make sequence changes, you'll find this logic tree a valuable reference. Parentheses in the upper right corner of each task card allow you total flexibility. They are left blank so you can pencil in sequence numbers of your own choosing.

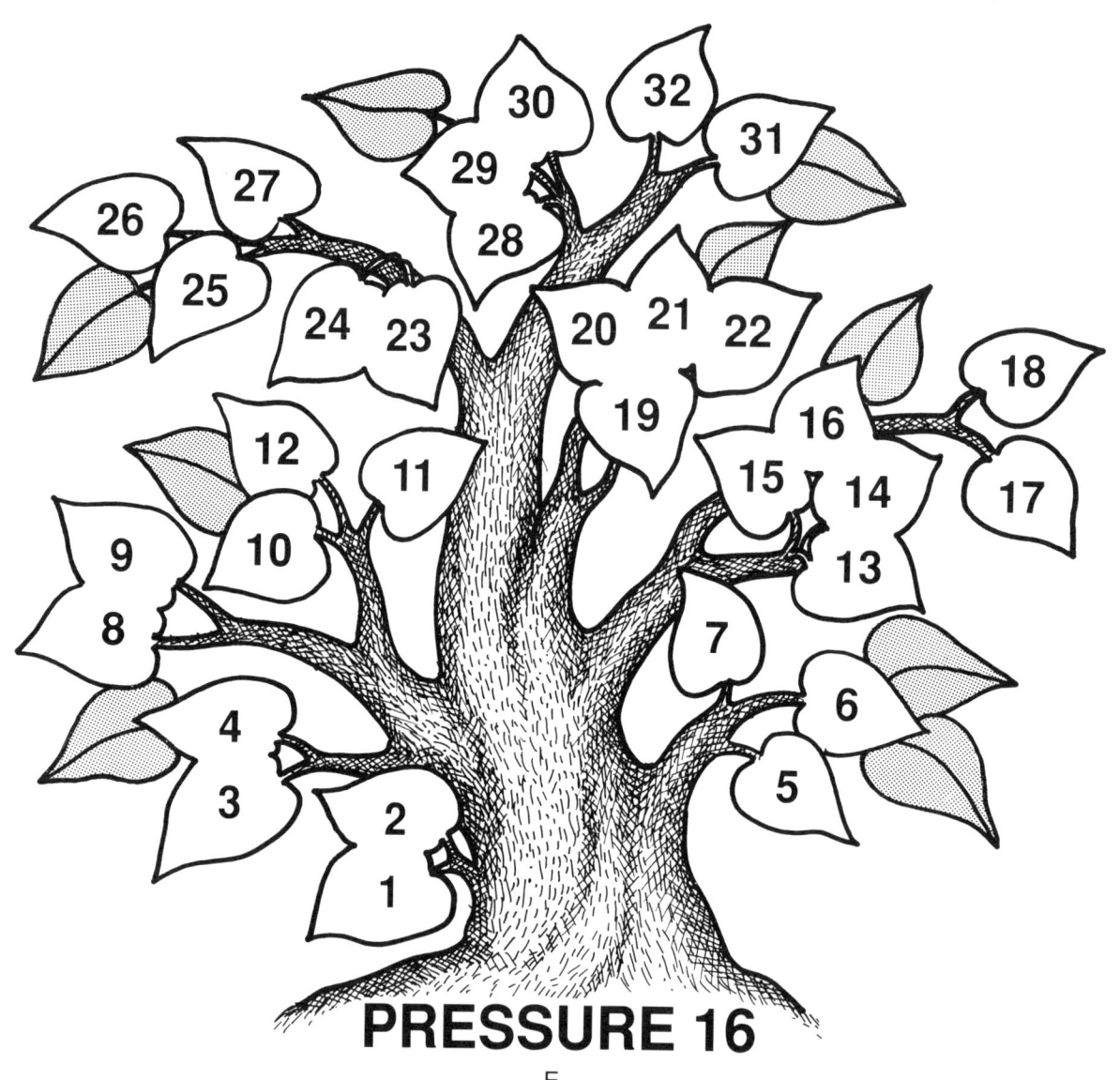

PRESSURE 16

E

LONG-RANGE OBJECTIVES

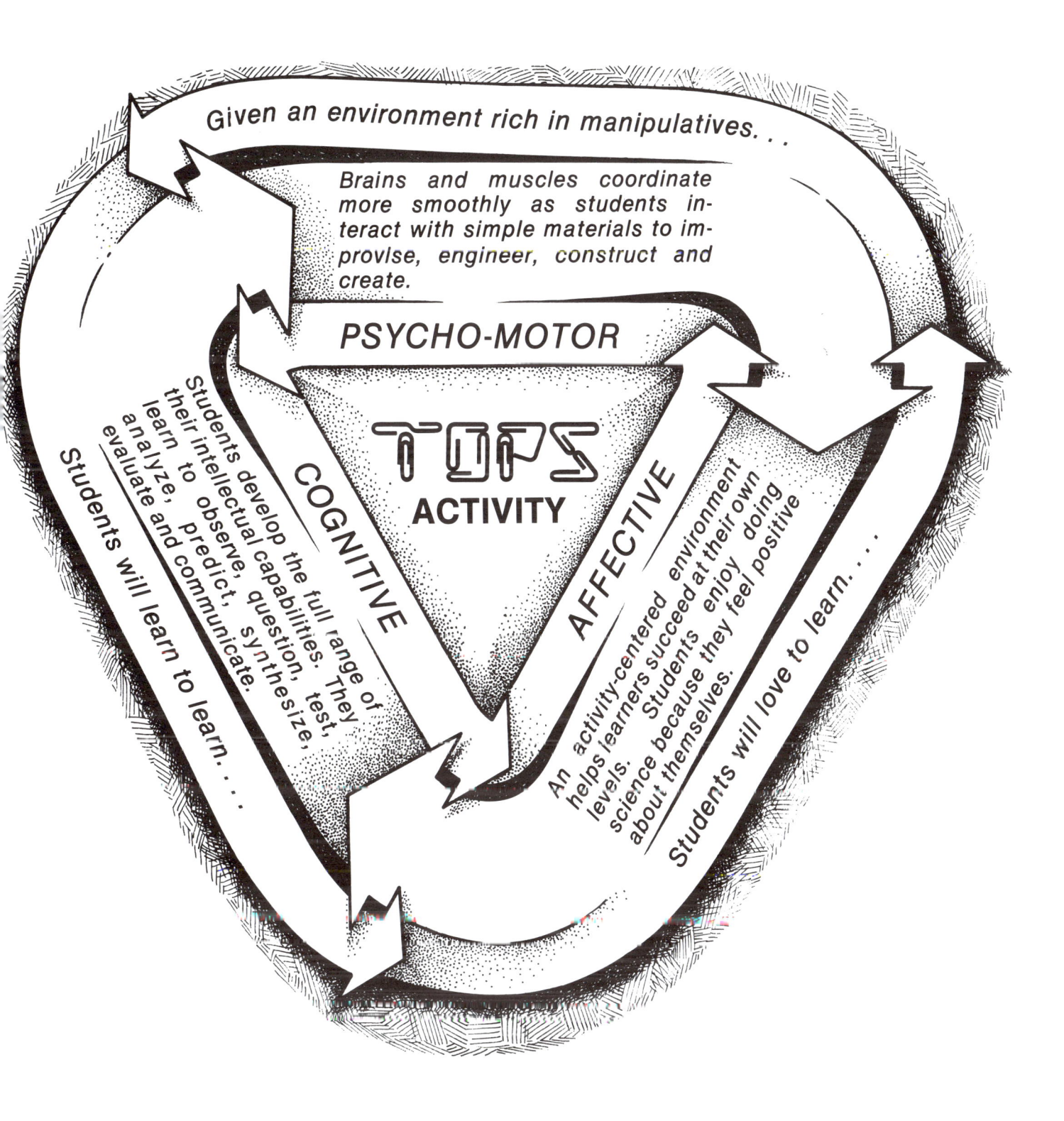

Given an environment rich in manipulatives...

Brains and muscles coordinate more smoothly as students interact with simple materials to improvise, engineer, construct and create.

PSYCHO-MOTOR

TOPS ACTIVITY

COGNITIVE

Students develop the full range of their intellectual capabilities. They learn to observe, question, test, analyze, predict, synthesize, evaluate and communicate.

Students will learn to learn....

AFFECTIVE

An activity-centered environment helps learners succeed at their own levels. Students enjoy doing science because they feel positive about themselves.

Students will love to learn....

Review / Test Questions

Photocopy the questions below. On a separate sheet of blank paper, cut and paste those boxes you want to use as test questions. Include questions of your own design, as well. Crowd all these questions onto a single page for students to answer on another paper, or leave space for student responses after each question, as you wish. Duplicate a class set and your custom-made test is ready to use. Use leftover questions as a review in preparation for the final exam.

task 1-2 A
The explorer knew at once she was in quicksand. With lightning speed she pulled off her backpack, then belly-flopped onto the brown ooze. Use concepts of force, area and pressure to explain how these actions enabled her to escape.

task 1-2 B
A 160 pound forest ranger owns a pair of boots (each with a bottom surface area of 40 square inches), and a pair of snow shoes (each with a bottom surface area of 480 square inches). Calculate how much pressure the ranger exerts against snow when wearing each kind of gear.

task 3
Explain how blowing up a balloon illustrates Pascal's principle.

task 3, 5
How would you use your head (and nothing more) to demonstrate that Earth's atmosphere exerts pressure?

task 1, 4, 6 A
Hand pumps **x** and **y** are both in good working condition. Which one is best to use…

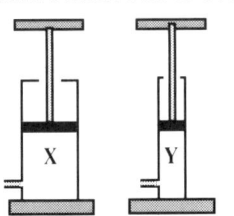

a. for inflating a skinny bicycle tire to a relatively high pressure? Why?
b. for inflating a large tractor tire to a relatively low pressure? Why?

task 1, 4, 6 B
Bottles **x** and **y** contain fizzy soda water under equally high pressure. Which bottle is more likely to pop its cork?

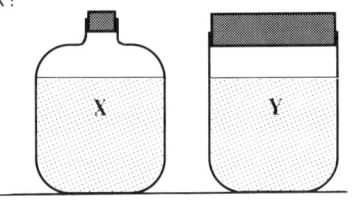

task 2, 5, 6 A
A postage stamp has an area six centimeters square.

a. If our atmosphere exerts a pressure of 10 N/cm^2, calculate the force pushing down on this stamp.
b. If all this force pressed down, why does a stamp need glue?

task 2, 5, 6 B
Atmosphere pressure pushes against this circle with about 10 N/cm^2.

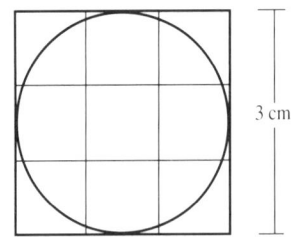

a. What is the pressure acting on 1 square? The force?
b. What is the pressure acting on the whole circle? The force?

task 7
Explain how atmospheric pressure helps you drink a glass of water with a straw.

task 7, 10
A gallon jug of water is inverted into a teacup.

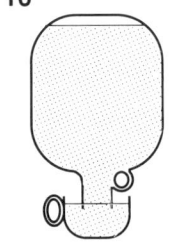

a. Why doesn't water spill over the top of the teacup?
b. How much water would you have to drink (with a straw) to fully empty the cup. Explain.

task 8, 16
A building contractor asks you to inspect a building foundation to insure that it is level on all sides. You say you and a helper can do the job using a garden hose and water. What will you do?

task 9
When you inhale a breath of air, does your diaphragm move up or down? Explain.

task 8, 10, 16, 17
You wish to clean a swimming pool that has no drain. Draw a diagram to illustrate how to siphon all the water out of the pool.

task 11-12
An inverted bottle, almost full of water, just barely floats in a swimming pool on space station Terra Twin. Rodney rests poolside, his body sinking into the lounge chair with artificial gravity set a Earth-standard 1. Suddenly his ears pop, sirens blare, and the bottle sinks. What happened?

task 9, 11, 12
What happens to this balloon as air is drawn out of the bell jar?

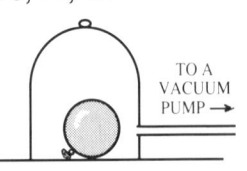

task 13-14 A
A jar of air is sealed to a U-tube manometer containing water.

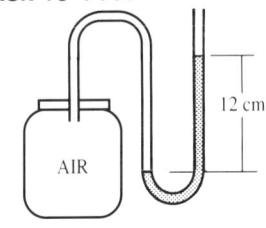

a. Is the jar pressurized or evacuated?
b. How much pressure is in the jar?

task 13-14 B
A jar of air is sealed to a U-tube manometer containing water.

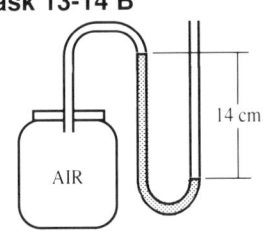

a. Is the jar pressurized or evacuated?
b. If atmospheric pressure currently supports 1033 cm of water, what is the total pressure in the jar?

Copyright © 1992 by TOPS Learning Systems.

Answers

task 1-2 A
The explorer minimized her pressure against the quicksand both by reducing her weight (throwing off the backpack) and increasing her surface area (resting on her stomach):

$$\text{Pressure}_{less} = \frac{\text{force}_{less}}{\text{area}_{more}}$$

task 1-2 B
$$P_{bts} = \frac{160 \text{ lb}}{40 \text{ sq in}} = 4 \text{ lb/sq in}$$

$$P_{snshs} = \frac{160 \text{ lb}}{480 \text{ sq in}} = .33 \text{ lb/sq in}$$

task 3
When you blow into a balloon, it forms a closed system with your mouth, throat and lungs. Increasing the air pressure in your lungs, by Pascal's principle, transfers this increase to all points in the system, including the balloon. This pressure change acts in all directions, pushing out the balloon in all directions.

task 3, 5
Suck air from your closed mouth to demonstrate that atmospheric pressure caves in your cheeks.

task 1, 4, 6 A
a. Inflate the bike tire to a high pressure with pump **y**. The small surface area of the plunger delivers maximum pressure for the force you apply:

$$\text{Pressure}_{high} = \frac{\text{your force}}{\text{small area}}$$

b. Inflate the tractor tire to a low pressure with pump **x**. The larger surface area of the plunger pushes maximum air per hand stroke into the tire:

$$\text{Pressure}_{low} = \frac{\text{your force}}{\text{large area}}$$

task 1, 4, 6 B
Bottle **y** is more likely to pop its cork. Its inside air exerts pressure across a much larger cork area than the air inside bottle **x**. Hence the larger cork is pushed with greater force.

$$P_{both} = \frac{\text{force}}{\text{area}} = \frac{\text{FORCE}}{\text{AREA}}$$

task 2, 5, 6 A
a. $\frac{10 \text{ N}}{\text{cm}^2} \times 6 \text{ cm}^2 = 60 \text{ N}$

b. The stamp needs glue because atmospheric pressure pushes in all directions, up as well as down.

task 2, 5, 6 B
a. Pressure = 10 N/cm²
   Force = $\frac{10 \text{ N}}{\text{cm}^2} \times 1 \text{ cm}^2 = 10 \text{ N}$
b. Pressure = 10 N/cm²
   Force = $\frac{10 \text{ N}}{\text{cm}^2} \times 7 \text{ cm}^2 = 70 \text{ N}$

task 7
Sucking on the straw lowers the pressure inside your mouth and straw. This allows atmospheric pressure, acting on the surface of the water, to push water up the straw.

task 7, 10
a. Water in the jug is supported by the weight of the atmosphere pressing on the surface of the water in the tea cup. This pressure acts in all directions, including upward.
b. Each time you lower the water level in the cup below the mouth of the jug, air enters, pressurizing the jug, and allowing more water to flow out. Thus, to empty the cup completely, you must drink all water in the jug.

task 8, 16
Run the garden hose between any 2 points you wish to compare, holding each end of the hose even with the top of the foundation. Pour water into the hose until it rises near the top of each end. Since water seeks its own level, it will define a level standard for judging the structure.

task 9
Your diaphragm moves downward to expand your chest cavity. This lowers the pressure surrounding your lungs, allowing outside air to flow inside and expand them into the enlarged cavity.

task 8, 10, 16, 17
To drain completely, the outflow must be lower than the bottom of the pool.

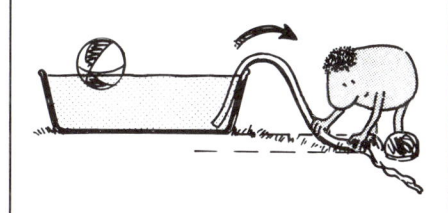

task 11-12
The space station has suddenly undergone an increase in air pressure. This acts everywhere within the closed system, forcing more water into the inverted bottle until it sinks.

task 9, 11, 12
Higher pressure air inside the balloon expands as the bell jar is evacuated, causing the balloon to swell.

task 13-14 A
a. The jar is pressurized.
b. Air pressure in the jar is 12 cm of water above atmospheric pressure.

task 13-14 B
a. The jar is evacuated.
b. pressure$_{atm}$ = 1,033 cm of water
   − pressure$_{man}$ =   14 cm of water
   pressure$_{jar}$ = 1,019 cm of water

Copyright © 1992 by TOPS Learning Systems.

Review / Test Questions (continued)

task 14
A balloon is inflated and tied. How will its size change as this balloon is carried...
a. high into the atmosphere? Explain.
b. deep into the sea? Explain.

task 15, 17 A
A U-tube and a straight tube both join in an inverted Y. Can you draw up water from level **a**, so both sides rest at level **b**? Explain.

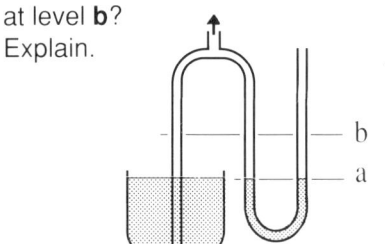

task 15, 17 B
A Y-tube with thick and thin arms is inverted in a jar of water. Can you draw up water from level **a** to rest in both arms at level **b**? Explain.

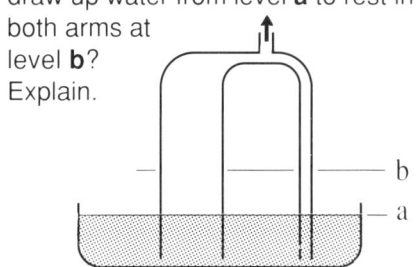

task 16-17
Why are city reservoirs built on towers or hills?

task 11, 16-18
Can thirsty Thad get a drink of water from this jar without removing the cork? Explain.

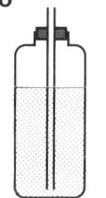

task 19-22 A
When you take a shower, the shower curtain tends to sweep in against you. Why does this happen?

task 19-22 B
Will this ball curve up or down? Explain.

task 19-22 C
Draw streamlines over this airplane wing to illustrate lift.

task 23-24 A
Water is boiled in a can to generate lots of steam. A lid is clamped on airtight, then it is cooled with water. What happens? Why?

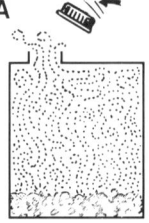

task 23-24 B
Burning paper is thrust into a juice bottle, and a peeled, boiled egg is placed on top. Hot expanding air pushes out past the egg, then the fire goes out. What happens next? Why?

task 25-26
Two glass tubes, one with a 5 cm^2 bore and one with a 1 cm^2 bore, are completely filled with mercury, then inverted into more mercury. The weight of each column is calibrated in Newtons.

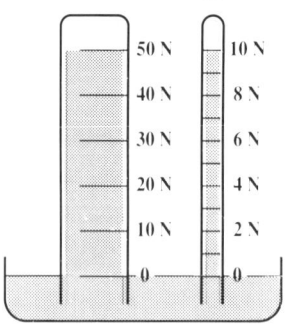

a. Do both tubes show the same outside air pressure? Show your work.
b. Why is there space at the top of each tube? What does this space contain?

task 25-27
The most powerful vacuum pump in the world cannot lift water higher than about 10.3 meters. Why is this so?

task 27
You have 2 test tubes, each with a hole in the bottom. One fits snugly inside the other, yet slides freely. How might you use these tubes and other simple materials to improvise a vacuum pump?

task 28-29
A graduated cylinder with a 7 cm^2 bore is filled with 105 ml of water. What pressure does this much water exert against its bottom?
(1 ml water weighs about .01 N)

task 28-30 A
Your space ship, pressurized at an Earth-like 2.2 lbs/cm^2 is punctured by a meteor in deep space.
a. Which way does air flow through the hole in your ship?
b. Can you plug this hole with your finger if it is pinhole size (.03 cm^2)?
c. Can you plug this hole with your palm if it is golf ball size (16 cm^2)?

task 28-30 B
This baggie can be inflated with a maximum lung pressure of .22 lb/cm^2.

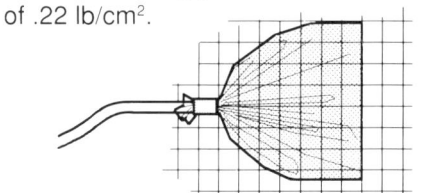

a. If every square represents 1 cm^2, what maximum weight can it lift?
b. Why does the baggie generally lift less than this?

task 31
a. Using a cut-off syringe and a cork, design an experiment to show how pressure changes with volume.
b. Using a heat-proof bottle and a cork, design an experiment to show how pressure changes with temperature.

task 31-32
a. Is this device a barometer? How does it measure changes in pressure?
b. Is this device a thermometer? How does it measure changes in temperature?
c. Can you take both measurements at the same time?

task 32
Is your U-tube manometer an aneroid barometer? Explain.

Copyright © 1992 by TOPS Learning Systems.

Answers (continued)

task 14
a. Atmospheric pressure decreases with height. As the balloon is carried higher, its inside air will expand outward, enlarging the balloon.

b. Water pressure increases with depth. As the balloon is carried deeper into the sea, outside pressure, pushing in from all sides, compresses it.

task 15, 17 A
No. If both sides rested at level b, the height of water in the U-tube would be twice as tall as in the straight tube. This is impossible, since both water columns are supported by a common pressure difference.

task 15, 17 B
Yes. Because each water column is supported by the same pressure, both must reach to the same height. Water height, not volume, is the variable that matters.

task 14, 16-17
Water pressure increases with depth. Reservoirs are built high above the city to provide higher pressure to city water pipes.

task 11, 16-18
Thad cannot drink water from the straw because the cork prevents outside atmospheric pressure from pushing up the water as he evacuates the straw. He can, however, increase air pressure inside the bottle by blowing bubbles through the water. When he stops blowing, this higher inside pressure lifts water up the tube and into his mouth.

task 19-22 A
As you take a shower, a stream of water and air flows past the inside of the curtain, creating lower pressure than the stationary air outside the curtain. This higher outside pressure sweeps the curtain inward.

task 19-22 B
Air passing above the ball moves *against* its spinning surface; air passing underneath moves *with* this spinning surface. Hence the air stream over the top is slower than over the bottom, creating higher pressure above, lower pressure below to curve the ball downward.

task 19-22 C

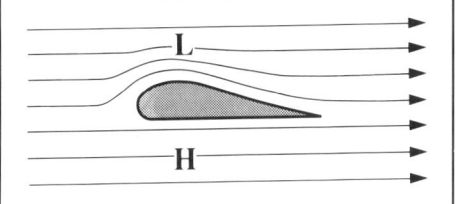

task 23-24 A
The steam inside the can condenses, creating a partial vacuum inside. Since no air can enter from outside to equalize this low interior pressure, the can is crushed, pushed in on all sides by higher atmospheric pressure.

task 23-24 B
The air cools and contracts, lowering air pressure inside the bottle. Higher atmospheric pressure, pressing in from outside, pushes the egg into the bottle.

task 25-26
a. Both tubes show the same pressure:
$$P_{thick} = \frac{F}{A} = \frac{50 \text{ N}}{5 \text{ cm}^2} = 10 \text{ N/cm}^2$$
$$P_{thin} = \frac{F}{A} = \frac{10 \text{ N}}{1 \text{ cm}^2} = 10 \text{ N/cm}^2$$

b. The space above each tube is a vacuum, containing nothing at all. Earth has just enough atmosphere to support a column of mercury this high, but no higher.

task 25-27
The best a vacuum pump can do is to create a perfect vacuum. Earth's atmosphere has sufficient pressure to push up water 10.3 meters into a perfect vacuum, but no further. No vacuum pump, no matter how powerful it is, can make Earth's atmosphere any heavier than it is.

task 27
Drop a loose fitting marble inside each test tube. Place the smaller inside the larger, lower both into water, and start pumping. On the up stroke, the bottom marble valve will open and the top marble valve will close: this drives water into the lower tube. On the down stroke, the bottom valve will close and the top will open: this drives water into the top tube. With continued pumping, water flows up through both tubes and out the top.

task 28-29
$$F = 105 \text{ ml} \times \frac{.01 \text{ N}}{\text{ml}} = 1.05 \text{ N}$$
$$P = \frac{F}{A} = \frac{1.05 \text{ N}}{7 \text{ cm}^2} = .15 \text{ N/cm}^2$$

task 28-30 A
a. Air flows from high pressure to low pressure, thus from the interior of the ship to the vacuum of space outside.

b. A pinhole can likely be plugged with a finger. The ship's atmosphere presses outward with very little force when applied to such a small area:
$$.03 \text{ cm}^2 \times \frac{2.2 \text{ lbs}}{\text{cm}^2} = .067 \text{ lbs}$$

c. A golf-ball size hole cannot be easily plugged with the palm. The ship's atmosphere presses with much more force over this larger area.
$$16 \text{ cm}^2 \times \frac{2.2 \text{ lbs}}{\text{cm}^2} = 35 \text{ lbs}$$

task 28-30 B
a. $\frac{.22 \text{ lbs}}{\text{cm}^2} \times 42 \text{ cm}^2 = 9.24 \text{ lbs}$

b. As you lift the load, some of the baggie's surface area bends around to increase its thickness. Those parts of the baggie that no longer contact the load can no longer lift it.

task 31
a. Plug the syringe with the cork. Decrease its volume until the cork pops off. This demonstrates the inverse relationship between decreasing volume and increasing pressure.

b. Cork the bottle and heat the air inside until the cork pops off. This demonstrates the direct relationship between increasing temperature and increasing pressure.

task 31-32
a. Yes. The water plug falls as the atmospheric pressure rises; it rises as the atmospheric pressure falls.

b. Yes. The water plug rises as the temperature rises; it falls as the temperature falls.

c. No. You must control one variable, either pressure or temperature, to reliably measure the other.

task 32
No. An aneroid barometer measures air pressure without liquid. The U-tube manometer contains water.

Copyright © 1992 by TOPS Learning Systems.

TEACHING NOTES
For Activities 1-32

Task Objective (TO) calculate pressures that squeeze clay when you stand on it. To observe how these pressures increase as your applied force is distributed over decreasing areas.

SQUEEZE PLAY — Pressure ( )

1. Roll a lump of clay into the size of a round Ping-Pong ball.

2. Sandwich it between 2 half pieces of index card, then squeeze it with the force of your own weight against a hard floor.

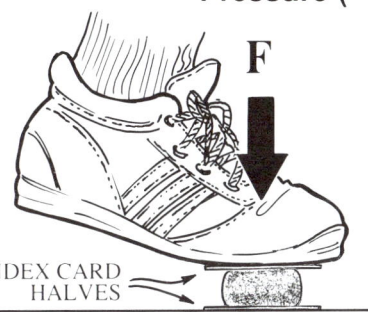

3. Use the Area Estimator (for Square Inches) to estimate the *area* (A) of your newly formed disk. Divide this into the *force* of your own weight (F) to find the *pressure* (P) that you applied.

$$P = \frac{F}{A}$$

4. Repeat steps 1-3 for marble- and pea-sized clay spheres. Save all three clay disks for step 5.

5. Relate the thickness of each disk to the pressures you have calculated.

6. You applied the same force to each lump of clay. Why, then, do the pressures change?

© 1992 by TOPS Learning Systems

Answers / Notes

3. Data and answers will vary. Here is one sample calculation: $P = \frac{F}{A} = \frac{170 \text{ lbs}}{4 \text{ in}^2} = 43 \text{ lbs/in}^2$

To estimate the area of a disk, simply center it on the concentric circles, then read its area at the circumference. If students are not using calculators, they should round off areas to the nearest whole number to simplify long division.

4. Marble: $P = \frac{F}{A} = \frac{170 \text{ lbs}}{1.5 \text{ in}^2} = 113 \text{ lbs/in}^2$ Pea: $P = \frac{F}{A} = \frac{170 \text{ lbs}}{0.6 \text{ in}^2} = 283 \text{ lbs/in}^2$

5. The thickest disk was flattened by much less pressure than the thinnest disk. The Ping-Pong disk, for example, was flattened to about 12 mm thick; the marble to 6 mm; the pea to 2 mm.

6. Pressures change as the constant weight of the body is applied over different areas. As these areas decrease, the smaller denominators divide into a constant numerator to yield larger quotients.

Materials

☐ A lump of clay.
☐ An index card.
☐ Shoes with relatively smooth soles. In step 2, students wearing track shoes or other "topographically enhanced" soles can step on an old paperback book to prevent lumps
☐ A pair of scissors.
☐ An Area Estimator for Square Inches. Photocopy this from the supplementary page at the back of this book.
☐ A bathroom scale (optional). Most students already know their own weight. Process is more important in this activity than accuracy.
☐ A centimeter ruler. Photocopy this from the supplementary page.
☐ A calculator (optional).

(TO) estimate pressures, in Newtons/cm², that one exerts while standing on the floor. To compare these pressures with Earth's atmospheric pressure.

PRESSURE PRINT

1. Outline the perimeter of your shoe on a Centimeter Grid.

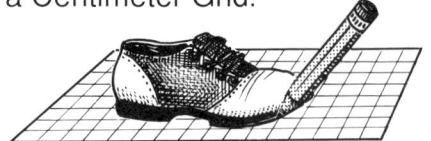

2. Estimate its area by counting centimeter squares. Count all squares greater than 1/2 as "one," all squares less than 1/2 as "zero."

3. Convert your weight from pounds to Newtons using this graph. What average pressure (in N/cm²) do you exert when standing on 1 foot?

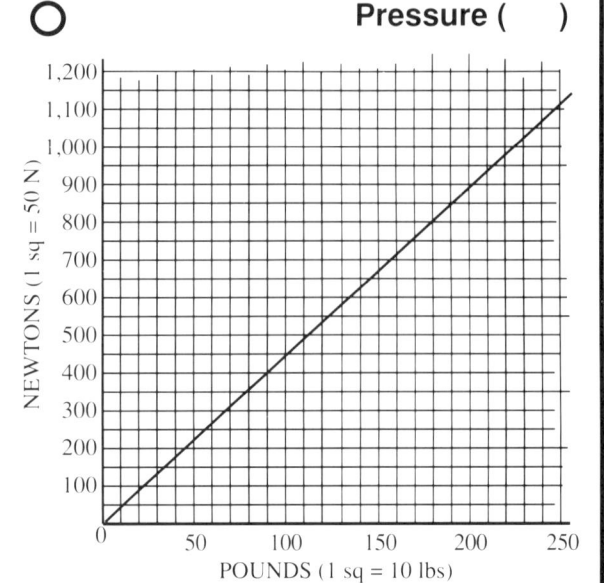

4. How does this pressure change when standing, with equal balance, on both feet? Explain your reasoning.

5. Earth's atmosphere exerts a pressure of about 10 N/cm² against the floor. Describe how you should stand to approximate this much pressure.

Pressure ( )

NEWTONS (1 sq = 50 N) vs POUNDS (1 sq = 10 lbs)

© 1992 by TOPS Learning Systems

Answers / Notes

1. *Students may remove their shoes or leave them on for this operation. Those with big feet must exercise creativity. They might splice two grids together with tape, or mark where the front of the sole leaves the paper, then trace the unmapped toe on another part of the grid.*

2-3. *The easiest way to count squares is to first cross out all those that have less than half their area remaining inside the print. Then count, row by row, all squares that remain.*

Here is one sample calculation:
Area of print = 252 cm²
Weight in pounds = 170 lbs
Converting to Newtons: 170 lbs = 760 N

$$P = \frac{760 \text{ N}}{252 \text{ cm}^2} = 3.0 \text{ N/cm}^2$$

4. Standing on both feet would distribute the same body weight over twice the area, thus lowering the pressure to half its former value. For the sample calculation above, this would be 1.5 N/cm².

5. To approximate atmospheric pressure against the floor, balance on the toe of one foot.

More advanced students should start with 10 N/cm², then work backwards to find the total number of toe squares necessary to support their particular weight at that pressure:

$$P = \frac{10 \text{ N}}{\text{cm}^2} = \frac{760 \text{ N}}{76 \text{ cm}^2}$$

This area, in particular, distributes body weight on the floor to make it equivalent to atmospheric pressure.

Discussion

Students will enjoy comparing foot pressures: Does a big foot make the deepest impression? Who walks most lightly?

Materials

☐ Centimeter Grid paper. Photocopy this from the supplementary page at the back of this book.
☐ A calculator (optional). A large denominator in the pressure calculation makes long division tedious.

(TO) feel a direct transfer of pressure between squeezing a bag and inflating your lungs. To understand that fluids transfer pressure changes to all points in a closed system; that these changes act in all directions.

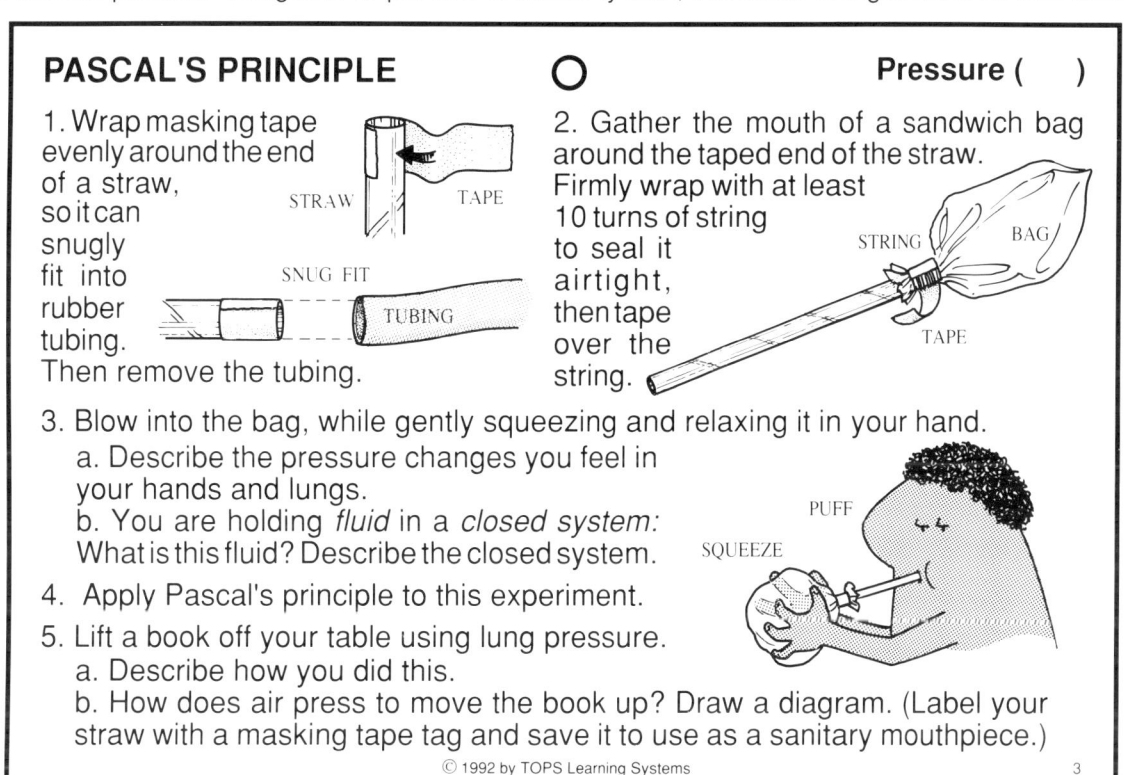

PASCAL'S PRINCIPLE   O   Pressure ( )

1. Wrap masking tape evenly around the end of a straw, so it can snugly fit into rubber tubing. Then remove the tubing.

2. Gather the mouth of a sandwich bag around the taped end of the straw. Firmly wrap with at least 10 turns of string to seal it airtight, then tape over the string.

3. Blow into the bag, while gently squeezing and relaxing it in your hand.
   a. Describe the pressure changes you feel in your hands and lungs.
   b. You are holding *fluid* in a *closed system:* What is this fluid? Describe the closed system.

4. Apply Pascal's principle to this experiment.

5. Lift a book off your table using lung pressure.
   a. Describe how you did this.
   b. How does air press to move the book up? Draw a diagram. (Label your straw with a masking tape tag and save it to use as a sanitary mouthpiece.)

© 1992 by TOPS Learning Systems

Introduction
Write Pascal's principle on the blackboard for your student to use as a reference in step 4: *A change in pressure at any point in a closed fluid system is transferred equally to all other points in that system, and acts in all directions.*

Answers / Notes
1. *To avoid spreading germs, every student should use a personal straw to blow into a personal plastic bag. Students should tag this mouthpiece by name to use in later activities that require mouth contact on tubes that are used in common with others in their lab group.*

3a. Squeezing the bag expands the lungs. Deflating the lungs expands the bag.

3b. The fluid is air. The closed system encompasses the bag, straw, mouth, throat and lungs.

4. As the bag is squeezed in the hand, this pressure change transfers equally to all other points in the closed system including the lungs. This pressure acts in all directions causing the lungs to inflate outward in all directions.

5a. Put a book on top of the plastic bag, then blow in air through the tube.

5b.

Materials
☐ Masking tape.
☐ Plastic straws with 1/4 inch diameter or slightly less. This fits into the 1/4 inch tubing, specified next, with just a little play. We find that straws usually sold in grocery stores must be wound with about 10 cm of masking tape to enlarge them enough to snugly fit into the tubing.
☐ Tubing with a 1/4 inch inside diameter and a 1/16 inch wall. Water tinted with food coloring must be visible in this tubing. This is true for clear plastic or natural rubber, but not black rubber. Each lab group requires 3 tubes to complete all experiments in this module. Cut them now to these sizes: 50 cm, 50 cm, 80 cm.
☐ A plastic sandwich bag.
☐ String.
☐ Scissors.
☐ A textbook.

(TO) experience how force increases as pressure is applied over larger areas. To observe how fluid systems give a force advantage at the expense of distance.

PRESS YOUR ADVANTAGE ◯   Pressure ( )

1. Fill a sandwich bag and a produce bag about 2/3 full of air. Attach them to your tube with string, as before, so the seal is airtight.

SANDWICH BAG — WRAP STRING 10 TIGHT TURNS — PRODUCE BAG 2/3 FULL OF AIR — TAPE OVER STRING

2. Squeeze air back and forth between the larger and smaller bags.
   a. Must you push with equal *force* to move the air between bags? Write your observations.
   b. Does the air in each bag press against the same surface *area*?
   c. Will squeezing one bag increase *pressure* in the other bag by an equal amount? Apply Pascal's principle.

3. Recall how pressure is defined. Do your observations in step 2 concerning F, A and P support this equation? Explain.

$$P = \frac{F}{A}$$

4. Use just 1 book to lift 2 books.
   a. Diagram how you did this.
   b. This machine gives you a force advantage. What is the disadvantage?

© 1992 by TOPS Learning Systems   4

Answers / Notes

2a. No. You must push the large bag with greater force than the small bag to move air back and forth between them.

2b. No. The air in the large bag pushes against a greater surface area than the air in the small bag.

2c. Yes. According to Pascal's principle, changes in pressure at any point in a closed system are transferred equally throughout that system.

3. Yes. A large force divided by a larger surface area in the large bag creates the same pressure as a small force divided by the smaller surface area in the small bag.

$$\frac{F}{A} = P = \frac{F}{A}$$
large bag   \   small bag
       same pressure

4a.

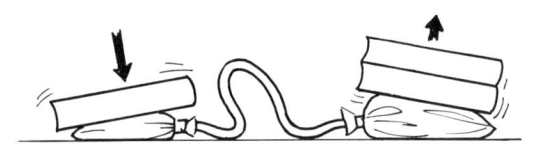

4b. The disadvantage is distance. Moving the single book down through a larger distance moves the heavier books up through a smaller distance.

These air bags plus other inventions that students construct throughout this module will be used again. Even though no "save" notice is given in the task cards, students should not disassemble their constructions unless specifically directed to do so.

Materials

☐ A plastic grocery produce bag. If you are recycling old bags, check for leaks before attaching. Small holes may be patched with tape.
☐ The 50 cm tube cut to length in the previous activity.
☐ String, scissors and masking tape.
☐ Three books of comparable size.

(TO) calculate the force of the atmosphere pushing against known areas. To feel the effect of this force when the equalizing pressure is partially reduced on the opposite side.

OCEAN OF AIR   O   Pressure ( )

1. We live under an ocean of air that exerts a pressure of about 10 N/cm² (2.2 lbs/cm²) at Earth's surface.

(circles labeled: 2 cm², 1 cm², 4 cm²)

a. How many Newtons of force are pressing on each of these circles right now? How many pounds?
b. If so much force acts on just these circles, why does this whole paper feel so light?

2. Tie string to a paper clip taped to the center of scratch paper resting on your table. Now jerk up on the string to lift the paper as fast as possible.

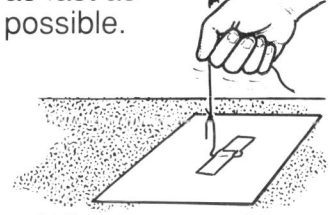

a. What happens?
b. Repeat the experiment with the paper resting on a canning ring.
c. What can you conclude?

3. Push a sandwich bag deep into a jar, then fold its top over the rim. Seal it airtight with at least 6 turns of string and hold the loose end.

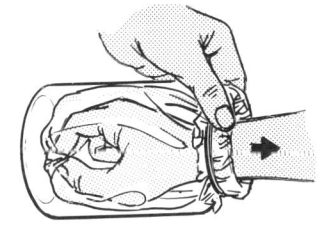

a. Why can't you easily pull out the bag?
b. Estimate the force (in both Newtons and pounds) that pushes in from outside the jar.

© 1992 by TOPS Learning Systems   5

Answers / Notes

1a. small circle:
$$\frac{10 \text{ N}}{\text{cm}^2} \times 1 \text{ cm}^2 = 10 \text{ N or } 2.2 \text{ lbs.}$$

medium circle:
$$\frac{10 \text{ N}}{\text{cm}^2} \times 2 \text{ cm}^2 = 20 \text{ N or } 4.4 \text{ lbs.}$$

large circle:
$$\frac{10 \text{ N}}{\text{cm}^2} \times 4 \text{ cm}^2 = 40 \text{ N or } 8.8 \text{ lbs.}$$

1b. The atmosphere presses against both sides of the paper, exerting pressure both upward and downward, as well as in all other directions. Hence, there is no net pressure holding the paper to the table.

2a. The paper tends to cling to the table, causing the string to tear off the tape and paper clip.
2b. With the canning ring beneath it, the paper more readily lifts off the table. The tape no longer tears loose.
2c. Lifting the paper very rapidly doesn't allow time for much air to flow behind the paper. Hence, the 10N/cm² pressure acting on the front of the paper is not equalized by as much pressure from behind.

3a. No additional air can enter the jar to equalize the pressure of the air pushing in.
3b. The mouth of a standard-sized canning jar has an inside area of about 30 cm²:

$$30 \text{ cm}^2 \times \frac{10 \text{ N}}{\text{cm}^2} = 300 \text{ N}$$

$$30 \text{ cm}^2 \times \frac{2.2 \text{ lb}}{\text{cm}^2} = 66 \text{ lbs}$$

If there were no air at all inside the jar (a perfect vacuum), the plastic would be held in the jar by all 66 lbs. But some air does remain inside. It, too, presses with a force of 66 lbs against the other side of the bag until you pull on the closed system, expand its volume, and thereby reduce the equalizing pressure.

Materials

☐ String and scissors.
☐ A paper clip and masking tape.
☐ A canning ring. Pick a size to match your jars — standard or wide mouth.
☐ A plastic sandwich bag.
☐ A glass jar that accepts canning lids and rings. Experiments in this module require at least 3 jars, 2 of which must be the same size. They should all have rings and lids that fit, plus at least 1 lid extra. Standard or wide-mouth jars both work. Limit your class to just one kind, if possible, to eliminate the problem of mismatched lids and rings.
☐ An Area Estimator (for square centimeters). Photocopy this from the supplementary page.

(TO) experience the full force of earth's atmosphere pressing against a vacuum. To observe how this force increases with increasing area.

SNAP AND POP   ○   Pressure ( )

1. Get a small syringe with no needle. Push the plunger fully in, then seal the other end with your finger. What happens if you pull the plunger…

   a. out until it separates from the barrel? Why?
   b. out halfway then let it go? Why?

2. Do you get the same results in step 1 if you leave the end of the barrel open? Why?

3. Consider two syringes with different diameters.

   a. If you sealed each one with your finger, would you expect to pull out each plunger using about the same amount of force? Make a prediction, giving reasons for your answer.

   b. Evaluate your prediction.

4. Use a syringe to show that Earth's atmosphere exerts pressure in *all* directions.

© 1992 by TOPS Learning Systems

Answers / Notes

1. The syringe makes a popping sound as the plunger leaves the barrel. This is caused by air rushing in to fill the vacuum.

1b. The plunger snaps back to its original position. There is (essentially) no air on the inside of the barrel to equally pressurize both sides of the plunger.

2. No. There is no popping sound, nor does the plunger snap back after you release it. Air was free to enter the barrel as you drew the plunger back, creating neither a vacuum nor unequalized pressure.

3a. No. Air pressing against the larger area of the big plunger pushes with greater total force, because it is applied over a greater area.

3b. As predicted, the plunger inside the large syringe requires more force to pull back than the plunger inside the small syringe.

4. Draw back on the plunger and point the syringe in any direction. When you release the plunger, it always snaps back with equal force.

Materials

☐ A small plastic syringe with about 3 cc capacity. These are sold over the counter in many drugstores. If they are by prescription only in your state, order from a scientific supply outlet or ask your local hospital for a donation of unused syringes. It is best if you can find a source without needles. If needles are attached, make sure you can remove them cleanly. Check to see that you can block the intake hole with your finger and draw back the plunger to form a good vacuum. Outside air should push it back to its original position. This is important here and in activity 26.

☐ A large plastic syringe with about 30 cc (or 1 ounce) capacity. (Feed stores may be a good alternate source for larger sizes.)

(TO) observe how atmospheric pressure acts in all directions, holding water inside a test tube. To use atmospheric pressure to transfer water with a straw.

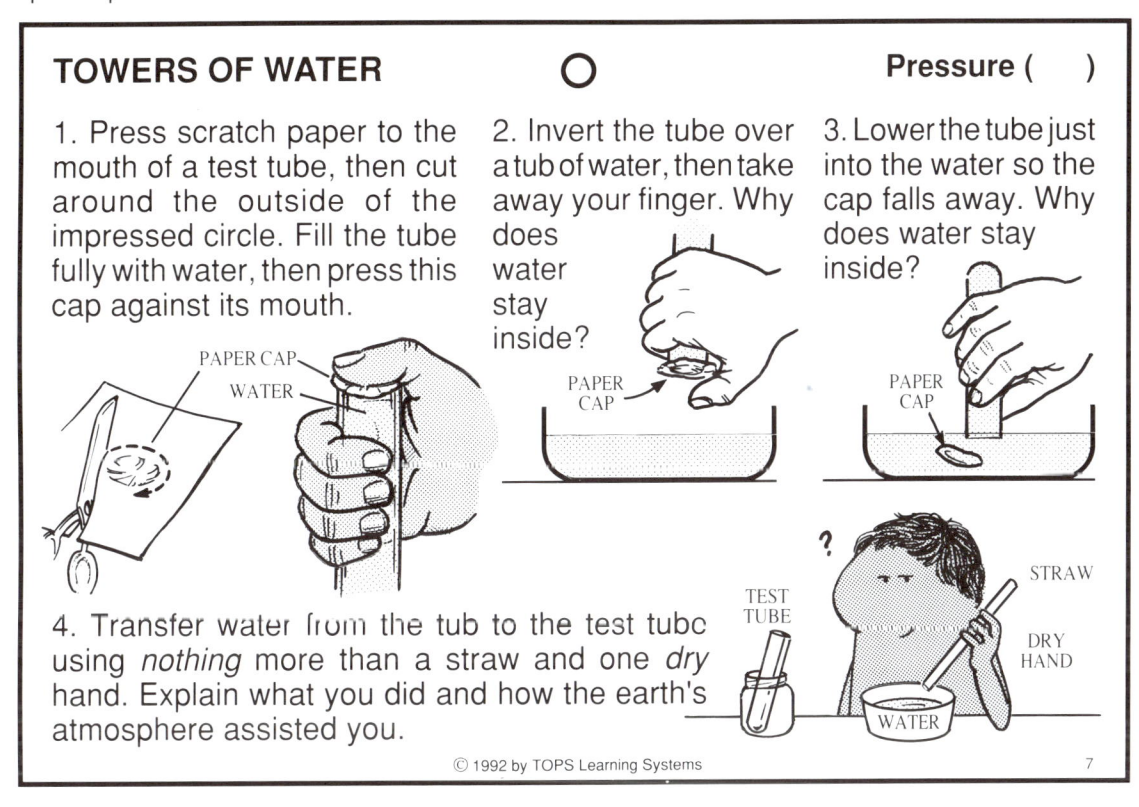

TOWERS OF WATER   O   Pressure ( )

1. Press scratch paper to the mouth of a test tube, then cut around the outside of the impressed circle. Fill the tube fully with water, then press this cap against its mouth.

2. Invert the tube over a tub of water, then take away your finger. Why does water stay inside?

3. Lower the tube just into the water so the cap falls away. Why does water stay inside?

4. Transfer water from the tub to the test tube using *nothing* more than a straw and one *dry* hand. Explain what you did and how the earth's atmosphere assisted you.

© 1992 by TOPS Learning Systems

Answers / Notes

1. *Notice how the atmosphere pushes the paper seal into a shallow concave curve. This forms the tightest seal.*

2. Water remains in the inverted test tube because the atmosphere, pressing in from all directions, has greater pressure than the water pushing out.

3. Atmospheric pressure applied to the surface of the water is transferred throughout the water in all directions, including upward into the tube. This is greater than the pressure of the water directed downward.

4. Put the end of the straw in water, then seal the top end with your finger. Lift the straw, hold it over the test tube, then release your finger to release the water. Atmospheric pressure keeps water inside the sealed straw, just as in the test tube. When you unseal the top, the atmosphere once again presses down as well as up. This allows the water to fall, by its own weight, out of the straw.

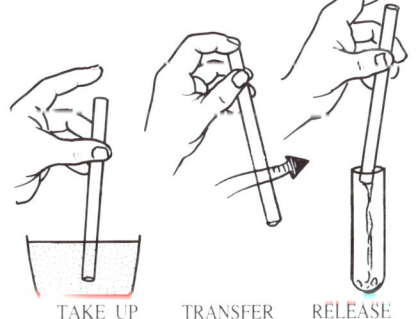

TAKE UP   TRANSFER   RELEASE

Demonstration

Find two test tubes with different diameters, so one fits easily, but not loosely, inside the other. Fill the larger tube with water. Invert it over the smaller, also inverted, to show how atmospheric pressure pushes the smaller up into the larger as the water drains out.

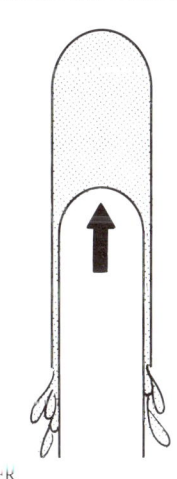

WATER

Materials

☐ A test tube. Any size will work, though large ones are more impressive.
☐ Scissors.
☐ Scratch paper.
☐ A large container. A dishpan, cake pan, large bowl or bucket all serve in many activities that require water-catching containers.

☐ A source of water. This is required in about half of the experiments in this module and is hereafter assumed. If you don't have a tap and sink in your room, maintain reservoirs in tubs or buckets.
☐ A small beaker or jar to transfer water and hold the test tube.
☐ A straw.

(TO) observe how water moves downward in response to gravity or upward in response to pressure. To construct a 1-hole cup for use in later activities.

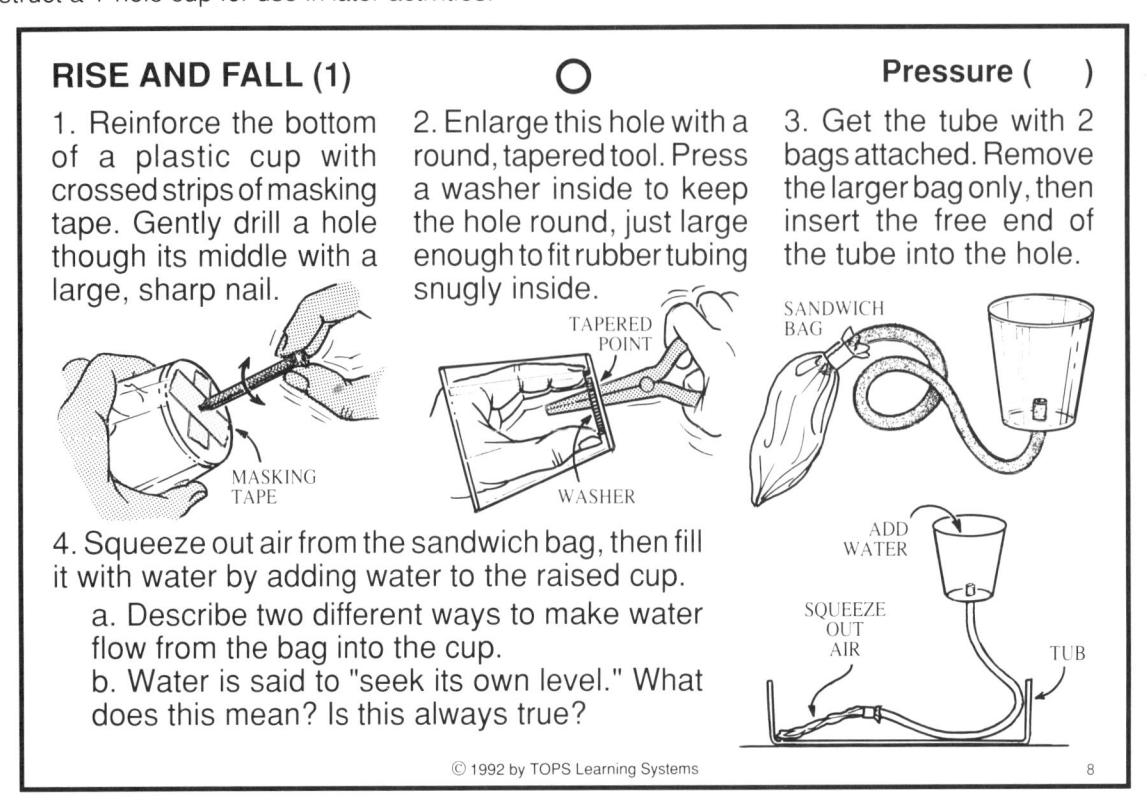

RISE AND FALL (1)   O   Pressure ( )

1. Reinforce the bottom of a plastic cup with crossed strips of masking tape. Gently drill a hole though its middle with a large, sharp nail.

2. Enlarge this hole with a round, tapered tool. Press a washer inside to keep the hole round, just large enough to fit rubber tubing snugly inside.

3. Get the tube with 2 bags attached. Remove the larger bag only, then insert the free end of the tube into the hole.

4. Squeeze out air from the sandwich bag, then fill it with water by adding water to the raised cup.

   a. Describe two different ways to make water flow from the bag into the cup.
   b. Water is said to "seek its own level." What does this mean? Is this always true?

© 1992 by TOPS Learning Systems

Answers/Notes

2-3. The tube should fit snugly, nearly airtight, because it has the same diameter as the washer which was used as a template.

4a. Make the water flow from the bag to the cup by squeezing the bag, or by raising it higher than the cup.

4b. Water flows from higher levels to lower levels until it is everywhere the same height. However, it flows to split levels, and remains there, when the lower water level is subjected to higher pressure – that is, when the lowered water bag remains squeezed.

Materials

☐ A clear cup made from soft plastic. Soft Solo brand cups work well. Check in advance to make sure you can drill a nail through the bottom without cracking the plastic.
☐ Masking tape.
☐ A large nail with a sharp point.
☐ Needle-nose pliers, a nail punch, or other round, tapered tool with a point small enough to fit a nail hole; the other end wider than the washer holes.
☐ Washers that fit snugly over the tubing detailed in activity 3. The center hole should measure 3/8 inches in diameter (this size washer is commonly sold to fit 1/4 inch diameter bolts).
☐ The 50 cm tube with attached bags from activity 4.
☐ A water tub. Though not specifically named in this activity card and others, its use is usually implied in the illustrations, and always listed in the materials section.

(TO) understand how the diaphragm regulates air pressure in the chest cavity, causing the lungs to expand and contract.

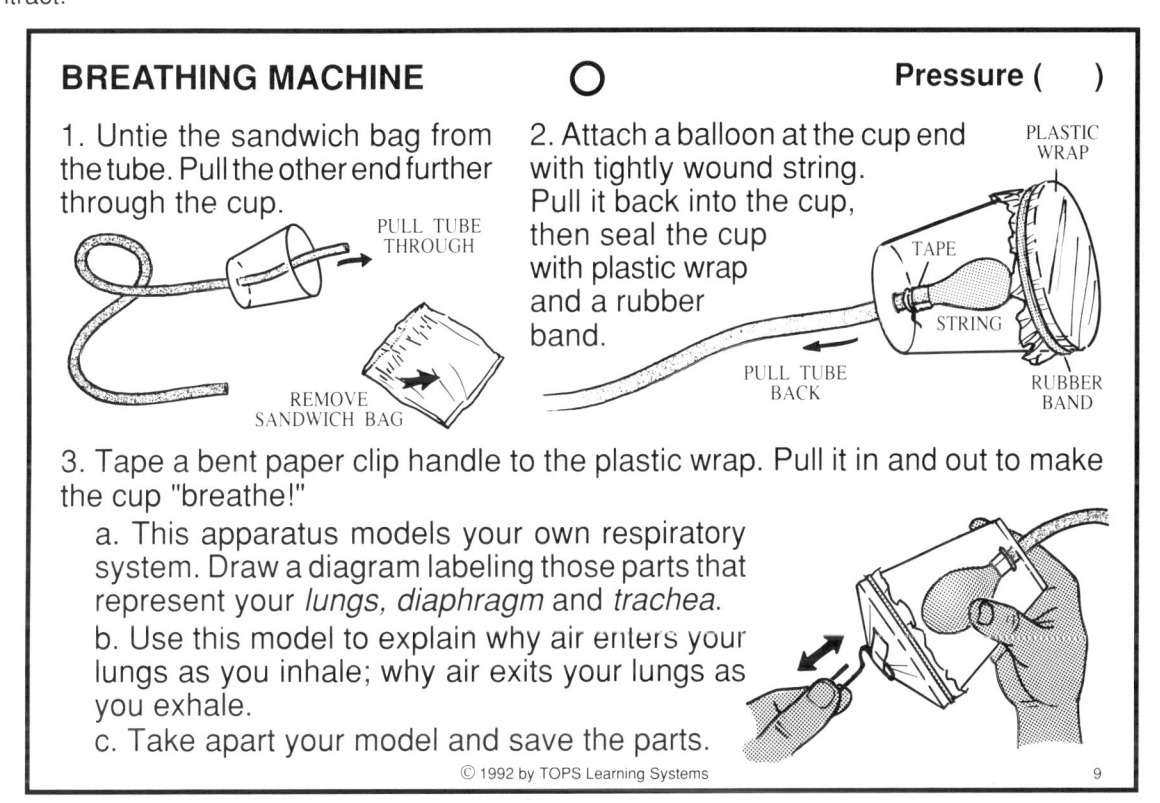

BREATHING MACHINE   O   Pressure ( )

1. Untie the sandwich bag from the tube. Pull the other end further through the cup.

PULL TUBE THROUGH
REMOVE SANDWICH BAG

2. Attach a balloon at the cup end with tightly wound string. Pull it back into the cup, then seal the cup with plastic wrap and a rubber band.

PLASTIC WRAP
TAPE
STRING
PULL TUBE BACK
RUBBER BAND

3. Tape a bent paper clip handle to the plastic wrap. Pull it in and out to make the cup "breathe!"

   a. This apparatus models your own respiratory system. Draw a diagram labeling those parts that represent your *lungs, diaphragm* and *trachea*.
   b. Use this model to explain why air enters your lungs as you inhale; why air exits your lungs as you exhale.
   c. Take apart your model and save the parts.

© 1992 by TOPS Learning Systems

Answers / Notes

3. *While most students will likely know how their lungs function, you may need to explain that the trachea is the "windpipe" into the lungs; that the diaphragm is a thin sheet of muscle beneath the lungs that contracts and relaxes to draw air into the lungs and release it.*

3a.

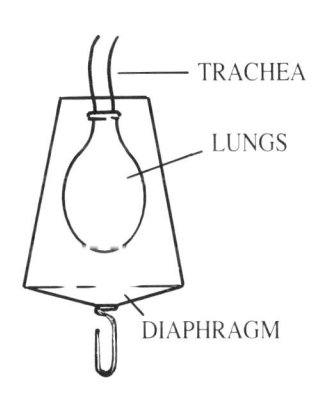

TRACHEA
LUNGS
DIAPHRAGM

3b. When you inhale, your diaphragm (the balloon membrane) moves downward, expanding your chest cavity (the interior of the cup). This lowers the pressure surrounding your lungs (the balloon). Atmospheric pressure causes your lungs to expand into your chest cavity to equalize this low pressure. Outside air is thereby drawn into your lungs.

When you exhale, your diaphragm moves upward to increase the pressure inside your chest cavity. This, in turn, compresses your lungs, which expels air until the pressures in your chest cavity and lungs are again equal.

Materials

☐ The tube, cup and bag assembly from activity 8.
☐ A small balloon
☐ String.
☐ Scissors.
☐ Plastic wrap.
☐ A rubber band.
☐ Masking tape.
☐ A paper clip.

(TO) support a column of water with atmospheric pressure, then siphon it down with gravity.

BUBBLES UP   Pressure ( )

1. Cover the bottom of a tub with about 2 cm of water, up to the first joint of your little finger.

2. Fill a jar brimful with water, cover with a canning lid, then invert in the water.

3. Slide the lid away, then raise the jar onto 3 washers. Be sure to keep its rim under water at all times.

4. Weigh down the end of a tube with washers. Suck water up through this tube, but pinch its end closed before the water reaches your mouth.

5. Release the water into a *lower* container or sink.
   a. What happens to the water? Fully describe what you see.
   b. What makes the water *siphon* (flow to a lower level)?
   c. The fall of water inside the jar is jerky rather than smooth. Explain why.

© 1992 by TOPS Learning Systems

Introduction

This is the first experiment where several students may wish to draw up water by mouth from a common tube. To avoid transferring germs, demonstrate the use of the straw mouthpiece constructed in activity 3: insert the taped end into the tube; place your mouth on this straw, and draw water through it. These sanitary mouthpieces are not specified in the activity cards, because individual students may have access to a dedicated set of tubes.

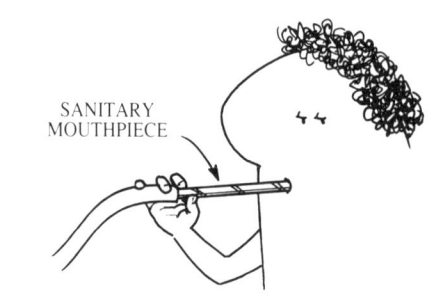

Answers / Notes

5a. Water flows (siphons) from the higher tub to the lower container, causing the water level in the tub to drop below the raised mouth of the jar. Air then enters the jar as a flurry of bubbles. This additional air increases the pressure inside the inverted jar, so more water flows into the tub and again seals the mouth of the jar. As water continues to drain from the tub, this process repeats until the jar and the tub empty to the level of the outflow tube.

5b. Water flows downhill under the influence of gravity. It is pushed uphill, over the rim of the tub, by atmospheric pressure.

5c. Water falls out of the inverted jar only in response to the increased pressure inside the jar, caused by air bubbling in. Because air enters the jar intermittently, rather than continuously, water falls out of the jar intermittently as well.

Materials

☐ A water tub.
☐ A canning jar with lid. The quart size is more impressive than the pint size, because it holds more water.
☐ A tube. If the 50 cm tube is not long enough to suit your apparatus, use the 80 cm length. This longer tube will later be used to construct a manometer.
☐ Washers that snugly fit the tube.
☐ A sink, bucket, or other suitable draining container.
☐ The sanitary straw mouthpiece constructed in activity 3.

(TO) apply Pascal's principle to a closed system, observing the effects of pressure changes in an eyedropper half full of water. To construct a 1-hole sealing lid for use in later activities.

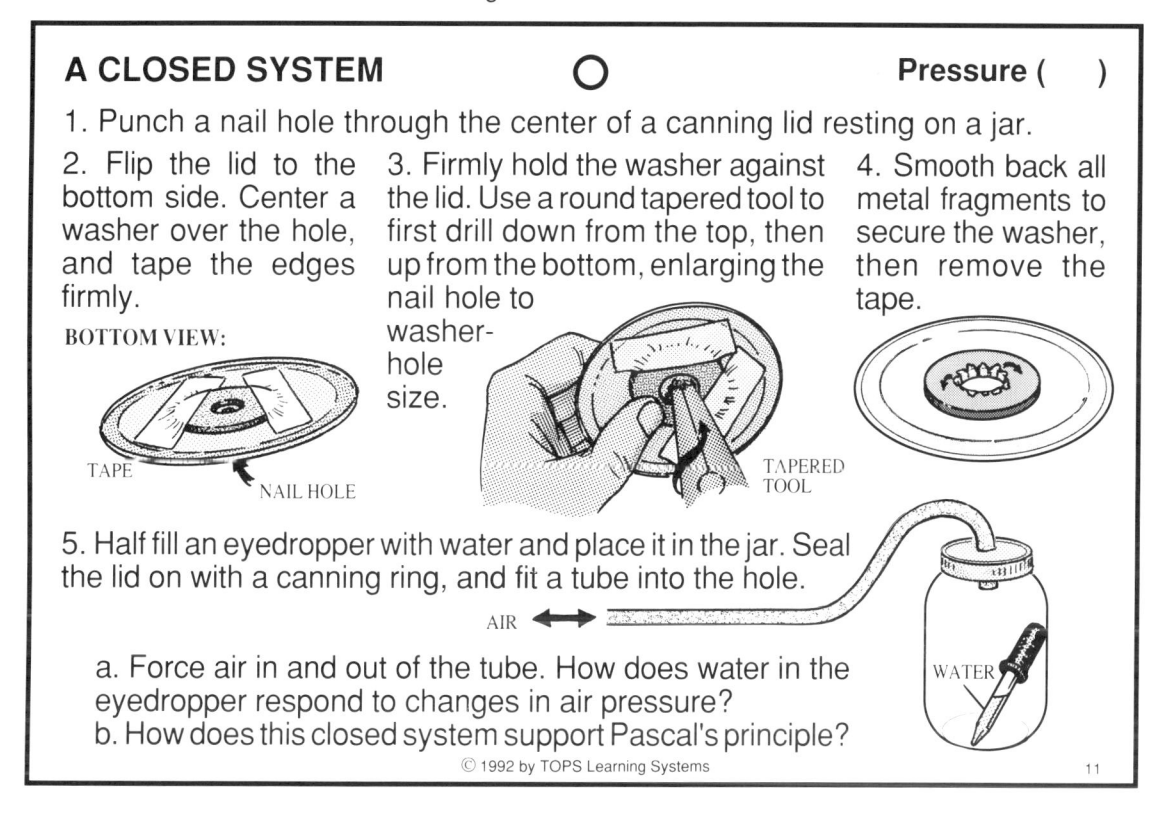

A CLOSED SYSTEM O Pressure ( )

1. Punch a nail hole through the center of a canning lid resting on a jar.

2. Flip the lid to the bottom side. Center a washer over the hole, and tape the edges firmly.
BOTTOM VIEW:
TAPE
NAIL HOLE

3. Firmly hold the washer against the lid. Use a round tapered tool to first drill down from the top, then up from the bottom, enlarging the nail hole to washer-hole size.
TAPERED TOOL

4. Smooth back all metal fragments to secure the washer, then remove the tape.

5. Half fill an eyedropper with water and place it in the jar. Seal the lid on with a canning ring, and fit a tube into the hole.
AIR ↔
WATER

a. Force air in and out of the tube. How does water in the eyedropper respond to changes in air pressure?
b. How does this closed system support Pascal's principle?

© 1992 by TOPS Learning Systems

Answers / Notes

2-3. *This tape anchors the washer firmly to the lid so the hole will not, inadvertently, be drilled larger than its washer template. If the washer is held firmly in place by the hand, the tape is not absolutely necessary.*

4. These fragments can be bent back and smoothed down with the drilling tool used in step 3 or the head of the nail used in step 1.

5a. Blowing air into the jar forces the water deeper into the eyedropper. Sucking air out of the jar pulls the water toward the tip, expelling some water from the eyedropper.
5b. Changes in lung pressure, in accordance with Pascal's principle, are equally transferred to all points in the closed system (mouth, tube, jar and eyedropper). Moreover, this pressure change acts in all directions, forcing water deeper into the eyedropper as lung pressures increase; drawing water out of the dropper as lung pressures decrease.

Materials

☐ A jar with new canning lid and ring.
☐ A large nail. Use this to drill the hole in step 1 by hand, or hammer it in with needle-nose pliers.
☐ Needle-nose pliers or equivalent.
☐ A washer to fit your tubing.
☐ Masking tape.
☐ An eyedropper.
☐ The 50 cm of tube.
☐ The sanitary straw mouthpiece.

(TO) explain the sinking and floating action of an eyedropper as water is forced in and out of the dropper by changes in water pressure.

SUBMARINE   Pressure (   )

1. Fill an eyedropper with enough water so it *barely* floats in a quart jar.
2. Using a canning lid (without holes) and a ring, seal this dropper in a quart jar *brimful* of water.
3. Press down on the lid to make your dropper dive. If it doesn't sink, draw a little more water into the dropper and try again.
4. The eyedropper sinks and floats as water moves in and out of it. Use Pascal's principle to explain why this happens.
5. Cut the head off a wooden match, leaving no excess wood. Float it in a test tube brimful of water, then make it sink and float by pressing with your thumb.
   a. What physical changes in the match head might cause it to rise and fall?
   b. Use arrows to diagram how pressure from your thumb is distributed through the water.

© 1992 by TOPS Learning Systems

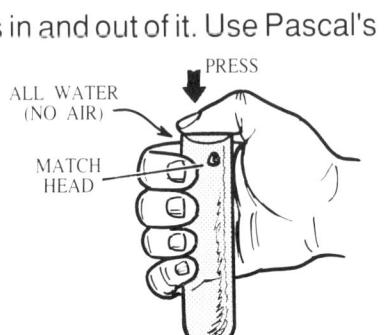

Answers / Notes

2. *Pressure changes travel relatively undiminished through incompressible water; but they are rapidly absorbed by compressible air. For best results, therefore, no air should remain in the jar, save that small amount trapped within the dropper.*

3. *Some trial and error may be necessary to reduce the buoyancy of the eyedropper to an absolute minimum.*

4. Pressing on the mouth of the jar increases the water pressure inside. According to Pascal's principle, this pressure change transfers to all points in the bottle, acting in all directions. Air inside the dropper compresses, allowing additional water to flow in until the dropper sinks.

Releasing the lid reduces this pressure, producing an opposite effect. Air inside the dropper expands, pushing out water until the dropper again rises.

5a. Air trapped in the head of the match contracts and expands, in response to changes in water pressure, causing the match head to sink and float.

5b. *Diagrams should suggest that pressure applied at the top of the jar is transmitted everywhere inside, in all directions.*

Materials

☐ An eyedropper. Those with glass barrels and simple bulbs can usually be sunk with water only. Screw-on droppers from bottles may require extra ballast (paper clips and a rubber band) unless the plastic bottle lid is temporarily removed.

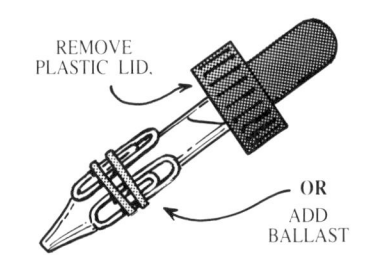

☐ A quart jar with an unpunctured canning lid and ring.
☐ A tub or equivalent container.
☐ Wooden matches.
☐ Scissors.
☐ A test tube.

notes 12

(TO) construct a U-tube manometer. To understand that it measures differences in pressure, not total pressure.

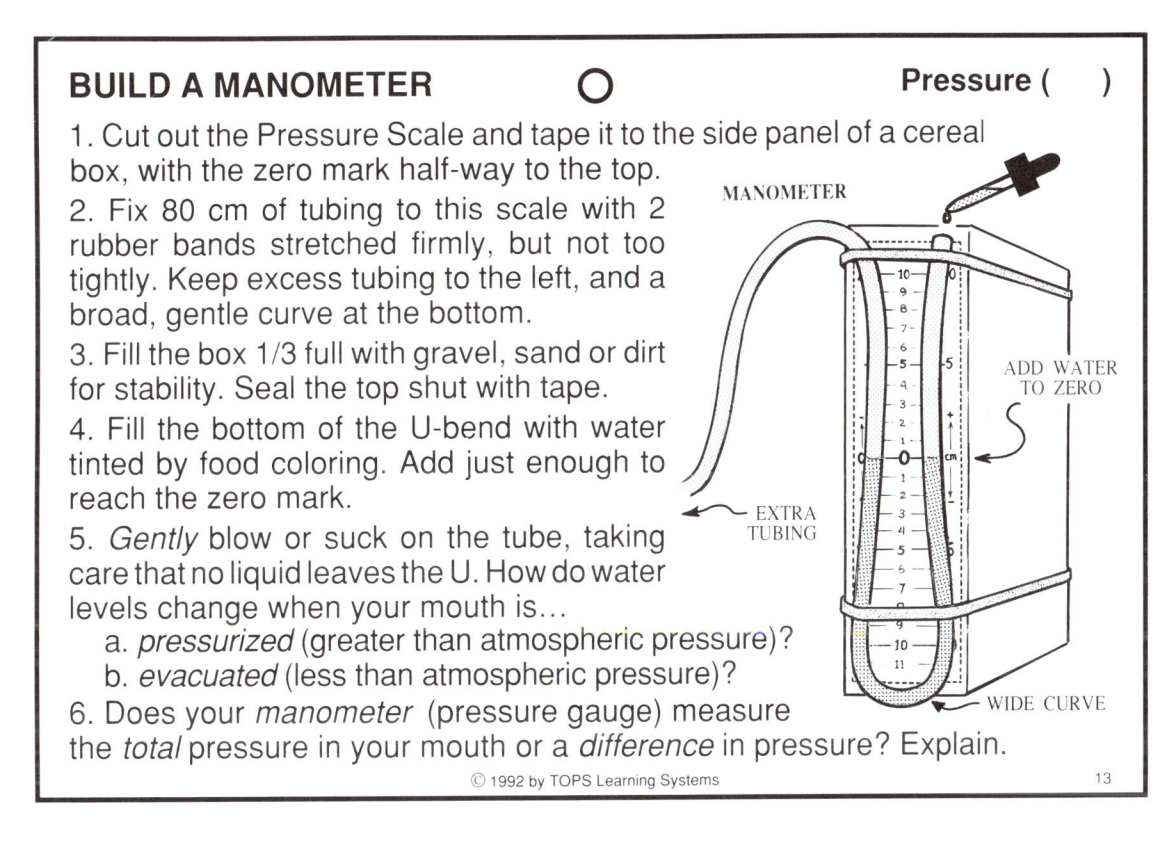

BUILD A MANOMETER — Pressure ( )

1. Cut out the Pressure Scale and tape it to the side panel of a cereal box, with the zero mark half-way to the top.
2. Fix 80 cm of tubing to this scale with 2 rubber bands stretched firmly, but not too tightly. Keep excess tubing to the left, and a broad, gentle curve at the bottom.
3. Fill the box 1/3 full with gravel, sand or dirt for stability. Seal the top shut with tape.
4. Fill the bottom of the U-bend with water tinted by food coloring. Add just enough to reach the zero mark.
5. *Gently* blow or suck on the tube, taking care that no liquid leaves the U. How do water levels change when your mouth is…
   a. *pressurized* (greater than atmospheric pressure)?
   b. *evacuated* (less than atmospheric pressure)?
6. Does your *manometer* (pressure gauge) measure the *total* pressure in your mouth or a *difference* in pressure? Explain.

© 1992 by TOPS Learning Systems

Answers / Notes

4. *Adding the water slowly, with an eyedropper, allows air to escape up the tube as water travels down. If air becomes trapped between additions of water, vigorously squeeze the tubing to expel it.*

5a. As the mouth is pressurized, water lowers on the left side of the U and rises on the right.
5b. As the mouth is evacuated, the opposite occurs. Water rises on the left side of the U and lowers on the right.
   For these reasons, the arrows on the pressure scale are identified with positive and negative signs as shown.

6. This manometer measures the difference between the pressure in your mouth and atmospheric pressure outside your mouth. At 0 cm, for example, the pressure in your mouth is equal to atmospheric pressure. There is no difference.

Materials

☐ Scissors.
☐ A Pressure Scale. Photocopy this from the supplementary page at the back of this book.
☐ A large cereal box.
☐ Clear tape. Or use pads of masking tape rolled sticky-side out.
☐ The 80 cm tube.
☐ Two large rubber bands.
☐ Sand, gravel or dirt.
☐ Colored water. Use enough food coloring to clearly show through your tube, but not stain it. Clear plastic tubing requires no coloring at all.
☐ An eyedropper.
☐ The sanitary straw mouthpiece from activity 3.

(TO) relate readings on the U-tube manometer to total pressure. To investigate the relationship between pressure and fluid depth.

CENTIMETERS OF WATER ○   Pressure ( )

1. Punch 2 holes through a canning lid with a nail. Use washers to get the correct spacing.
2. Drill out each hole with a washer underneath, as you did in activity 11.
3. Connect your manometer plus a second tube to a jar. Seal all joints airtight with grease.
4. Evacuate the jar 4 cm *from zero*. Hold this pressure with a clothespin throughout this step.
    a. Is your system airtight? How do you know? If not, fix it.
    b. What is the *difference* in air pressure, measured in cm of water, inside and outside the jar?
    c. If you could pump every last molecule of air out of your jar to create a *perfect vacuum*, the water levels (in a manometer very much taller than this one) would separate 1034 cm! How high does 1034 cm reach?
    d. If the atmosphere supports 1034 cm of water, what is the *total* pressure now in your jar?
5. Take off the clothespin, then place the end of the tube into a jar of water.
    a. How does water pressure change with depth?
    b. Do you think this relationship holds for other fluids, like air? Explain.

© 1992 by TOPS Learning Systems   14

Introduction

Demonstrate how to use petroleum jelly to make an airtight seal: Coat around the outside of the tube just before it is inserted to the required depth. Then push the tube into final position so grease fills up the circular joint.

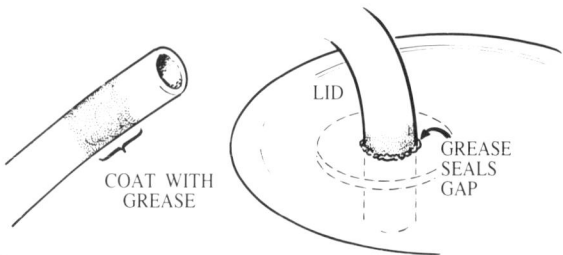

Answers / Notes

1. *Students should keep enough space between the holes to accommodate both washers.*

4a. *The system is airtight if the water levels hold at 4 cm above and below zero. (If students do detect movement, they should regrease all joints, including the lid seal, then evacuate their system and evaluate it again.)*

4b. *Air pressure inside the jar is 8 cm of water lower than atmospheric pressure outside the jar.*

4c. *1034 centimeters reaches 10.3 meters, or 34 feet. This is about as tall as a 3-story building.*

4d. *Total atmospheric pressure equals 1034 cm of water. Since the pressure inside the jar is 8 cm less, it must have a total pressure of 1026 cm of water.*

5a. *As the end of the tube sinks deeper into the water, the manometer registers a corresponding increase in pressure. Thus, pressure increases with depth.*

5b. *Yes. Pressure increases with depth in air as well as in water. Descending many floors in an elevator, in an airplane, or down a mountain in a car, increases the outside air pressure on your eardrums. You feel this pressure difference until yawning or swallowing makes them "pop", equalizing the pressure inside and out.*

Materials

- ☐ A jar with new canning lid and ring.
- ☐ A large nail.
- ☐ Needle-nose pliers or other tapered tool.
- ☐ Washers that fit your tubing.
- ☐ Masking tape.
- ☐ The manometer previously constructed.
- ☐ The 50 cm tube.
- ☐ The sanitary straw mouthpiece.
- ☐ A jar of petroleum jelly.
- ☐ A clothespin.

(TO) discover that atmospheric pressure supports the same difference in water levels in both straight tubes and U-tubes. To observe that height, not volume, is the variable that matters.

U TUBE / STRAIGHT TUBE   Pressure ( )

1. Construct a 3-hole lid with washers, similar to your 1-hole and 2-hole lids.

2. Attach 2 tubes plus your manometer with air-tight seals. Feed one of the tubes through the top rubber band of your manometer, then down into a small jar of tinted water.

3. Gently evacuate the large jar. Notice that it is now connected to *two* different manometers.
   a. How is the new manometer different?
   b. Do they both indicate the same pressure?
   c. Where is the water in each manometer exposed to Earth's atmosphere?

4. Replace the small jar of colored water with a pie tin half full of clear water. Connect your 1-hole cup to the tube, and seal airtight.
   a. Does each gauge still register the same pressure?
   b. Should pressure be measured by the *volume* of water it supports, or its *height*? Explain.

© 1992 by TOPS Learning Systems

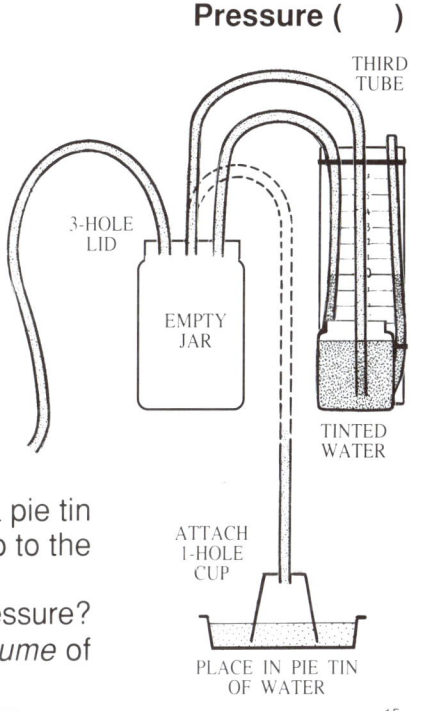

Answers / Notes

3. *If you tried to measure positive pressures with this straight-tube manometer, you would only blow bubbles. This is possible, however, with a much deeper jar, clear plastic tubing and clear water.*

3a. The new manometer consists of a straight tube lowered into a jar of water, rather than a U-tube half filled with water.

3b. Yes, both manometers give the same readings. The height of the water column above the surface of the water in the small jar always equals the difference in water levels in the U-tube.

3c. Earth's atmosphere exerts pressure on the surface of the water in the small jar to force it up the straight tube. It exerts pressure on the surface of the water in the right arm of the U-tube to force it down the right arm and up the left.

4a. Yes. The rise of water in the cup still equals the difference in water levels in the U tube.

4b. Pressure cannot be measured by volume because the same atmosphere pushed much more water up inside the cup than into the U-tube. Yet the heights in both manometers were equal. Height, not volume, is the decisive variable.

While the force needed to lift a large volume of water is greater, it is distributed over a proportionally larger area. Hence the pressure that supports each column, large or small, is the same.

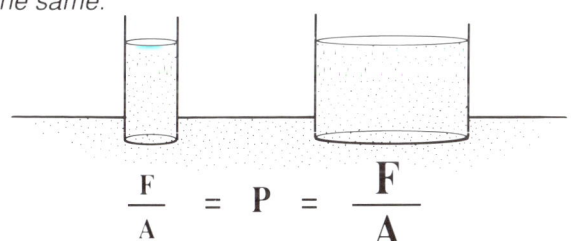

$$\frac{F}{A} = P = \frac{F}{A}$$

Materials

☐ A jar with new canning lid and ring.
☐ A large nail.
☐ Needle-nose pliers or other tapered tool.
☐ Washers to fit the tubing.
☐ Masking tape.
☐ Two 50 cm tubes.
☐ The manometer constructed in activity 13.
☐ A jar of petroleum jelly.
☐ A small beaker or baby food jar.
☐ Water tinted with food coloring.
☐ A centimeter ruler.
☐ A pie tin.
☐ The 1-hole cup from activity 8.
☐ The sanitary straw mouthpiece.

(TO) observe how water flows in response to changes in pressure or gravity. To understand that it seeks is own common level, unless supported by a difference in pressures.

RISE AND FALL (2) ○   Pressure ( )

1. Half-fill two jars of water. Seal the left with a 2-hole lid; the right with a 3-hole lid.
2. Run a connecting tube into the bottom of each jar. Close off the remaining hole on the left jar with a second tube pushed just a little inside.
3. Think of an *easy* way to fill the middle tube with water. Write your prediction first, then test it.
4. How many different ways can you make water flow from one jar to the other? Describe them all.
5. Remove the left tube. Cover its hole tightly with your finger, then set the right jar on an inverted can.
   a. Why doesn't the water seek its own level?
   b. If normal atmospheric pressure is **A**, and the difference in water levels is **h**, what is the pressure, **P**, in each jar?
   c. Use your manometer to see if your answer in b is correct. (You may need to grease both left holes airtight.)

© 1992 by TOPS Learning Systems   16

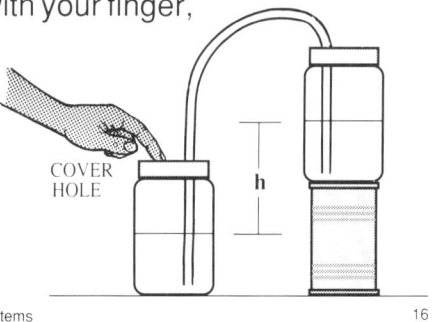

Answers / Notes

3. Blow air into the left jar to increase its inside pressure. This will force water up the tube and into the right jar, which is still under lower atmospheric pressure.

   This is actually what happens. *(Water remains in the tube thereafter, connecting the water in both jars.)*

4. Water will flow from one jar to the other in response to pressure or gravity:

   pressure: raise the pressure inside the left jar by blowing air into the tube to shift the water right; lower its pressure by sucking air out of the tube to shift the water left.

   gravity: raise the left jar above the right to shift the water right; lower the left jar below the right to shift the water left.

5a. The water remains at a higher level in the right jar because it is supported by a pressure that is higher than atmospheric pressure in the left jar.
5b. **P = A** in the higher right jar; **P = A + h** in the lower left jar.
5c. As predicted, the pressure in the left jar is higher than the right by a difference of **h** cm. That is, the difference in water levels in the two jars equals the difference in water levels in the manometer.

Materials

☐ Two equal-sized canning jars, quart or pint capacity.
☐ A 2-hole lid and 3-hole lid with accompanying rings.
☐ The two 50 cm tubes.
☐ The sanitary straw mouthpiece.
☐ A medium-sized can.
☐ Petroleum jelly.
☐ The improvised manometer.
☐ A metric ruler.

Demonstration

This demonstration is best used to reinforce concepts in Activity 17.

Cut off and discard the rounded end of a small balloon. Use the neck end to join a long piece of tubing (the longer, the better) to a 1 gallon plastic milk jug full of water. Secure the connections tightly with string.

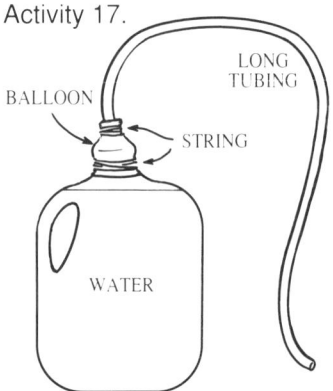

Discuss what will happen if you invert the jug over a sink. *(Water will drain out while the atmosphere slowly crushes the jug.)*

Does it matter how long the tube is? *(Yes. The difference in pressure inside and outside the jug is measured by the difference in water levels it must support. The longer the tube, the greater this difference.)*

(TO) reinforce the idea that water height, not volume, determines pressure.

RISE AND FALL (3) ○ Pressure (   )

1. Fill a jar half full of water and seal it with your two-hole lid. Insert 2 tubes into the holes as shown. Attach your 1-hole plastic cup to the tube that extends to the bottom of the jar.
   a. Raise the pressure in the jar below, until you fill the cup above. Does it matter how high you hold the cup? Explain.
   b. What is the maximum pressure, in cm of water, that the higher cup exerts on the lower jar?
   c. Can you control the flow of water from jar to cup without changing the air pressure? Explain.

2. Push the other tube below the water so *both* touch the bottom of the jar. Grease both lid holes to assure an airtight seal.
   a. Raise the pressure in the lower jar once more. What happens differently? Cite 3 differences, explaining each one.
   b. Use this apparatus to show that *height,* not *volume,* is the appropriate variable to measure pressure.

© 1992 by TOPS Learning Systems

Answers / Notes

1a. The higher you raise the cup, the more lung pressure is required to lift water into it.

1b. Students should measure the difference in water levels in a fully raised cup. This will be about 50 cm of water.

It is interesting to note that doubling the mass of air in the jar doubles its pressure to 2 atmospheres. This much pressure would push the water about 1,030 cm (10.3 meters) up a tube, if you could find one long enough. This much pressure is what a scuba diver feels at a depth of 10.3 meters.

On the other hand, the pressure normally found in an open jar (1 atmosphere) will also push a water column to this same height as you evacuate all the air from the 10.3 meter tube. This tube must be stronger than rubber, which would collapse as outside atmospheric pressure pushed in from all sides.

1c. Yes. You can control the flow of water by gravity. Simply lower the cup below the water level in the jar, and water will run into it. *(The connecting tube, of course, must be filled with water, not air.)*

2a. (1) Air now bubbles through the water as you pressurize the jar. This is because the mouth of the intake tube is now submerged.

(2) Water raised into the cup remains there, after removing your mouth from the intake tube. It is supported by the higher air pressure in the lower jar. With the mouth of the intake tube now under water, excess air can't escape.

(3) Water also rises into the intake tube just as high as in the raised cup. Both "towers" of water are supported by the higher pressure in the lower jar.

2b. Force water into the raised cup until it is nearly full, then lower and raise the end of the tube you just blew through. Water will spill out of the intake tube just as you lower it below the water level in the raised jar. Both water columns reach to the same height, even though the cup contains a far greater volume of water. Water height, not volume, determines pressure.

Materials

☐ A canning jar with 2-hole lid and ring.
☐ Petroleum jelly.
☐ Two 50 cm tubes.
☐ The 1-hole plastic cup.
☐ A tub or equivalent container.
☐ The sanitary straw mouthpiece.
☐ A centimeter ruler.

(TO) analyze a fluid system that is driven by continuous changes in pressure.

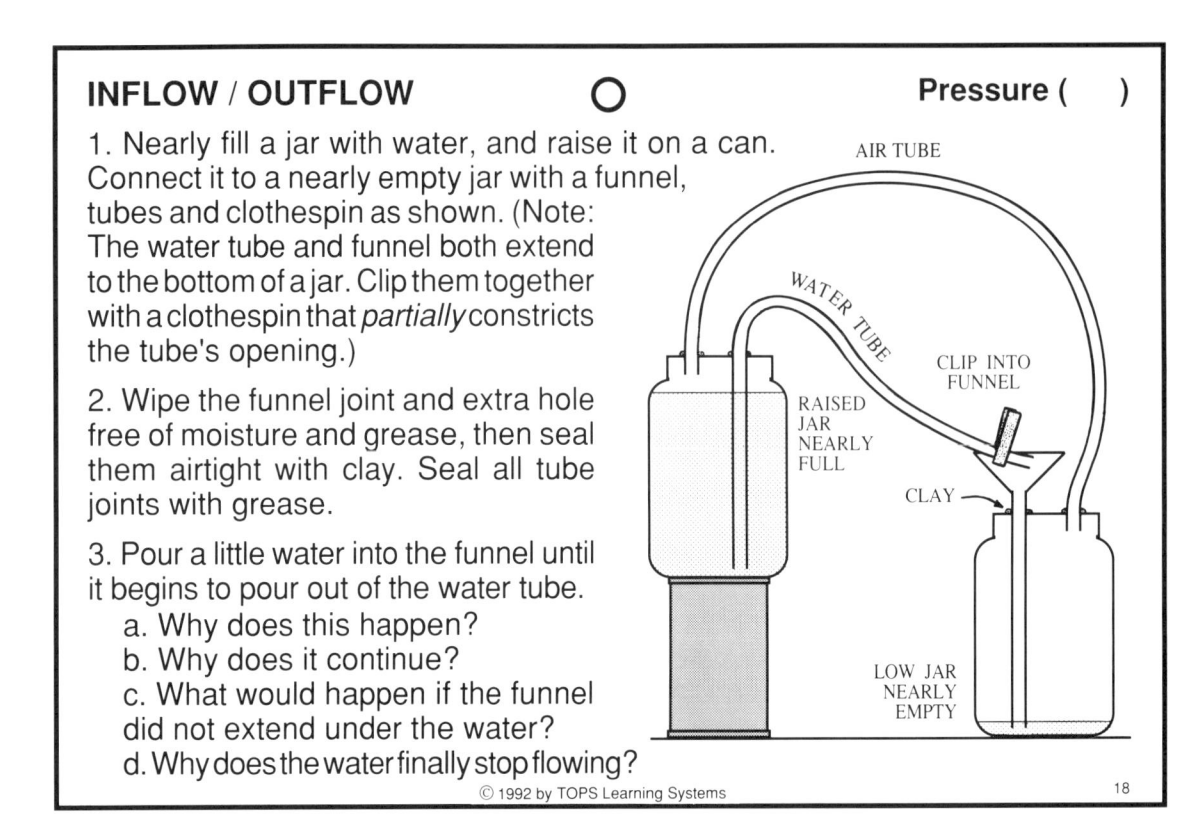

INFLOW / OUTFLOW   Pressure ( )

1. Nearly fill a jar with water, and raise it on a can. Connect it to a nearly empty jar with a funnel, tubes and clothespin as shown. (Note: The water tube and funnel both extend to the bottom of a jar. Clip them together with a clothespin that *partially* constricts the tube's opening.)

2. Wipe the funnel joint and extra hole free of moisture and grease, then seal them airtight with clay. Seal all tube joints with grease.

3. Pour a little water into the funnel until it begins to pour out of the water tube.
   a. Why does this happen?
   b. Why does it continue?
   c. What would happen if the funnel did not extend under the water?
   d. Why does the water finally stop flowing?

© 1992 by TOPS Learning Systems

Answers / Notes

3. *Trouble shooting: If the funnel does not hold its water, there is a leak in one or both jars. Pinch the interconnecting air tube temporarily closed to test for leaks in the bottom jar only. This is most likely, since the clay seals are prone to leak if applied to wet or greasy surfaces.*

3a. Some water flows through the funnel into the sealed jar below. This raises its pressure to a point where it resists further inflow, supporting a column of water in the funnel to perhaps 10 cm high. This increased pressure transfers to all points within both jars, since they are interconnected by an air tube. This pressure, in turn, forces water up the water tube and out into the funnel.

3b. Water flows *out of* the raised jar and up through its water tube, thus relieving the pressure build-up in both jars. At the same time, additional water flows *into* the lower jar, through the funnel, thus raising the pressure in both jars. This outflow and inflow maintains a positive net pressure, which continues to drive the system.

3c. If the stem of the funnel did not extend under the water, there could be no build-up of pressure to drive water up into the funnel. Air, instead, would flow up through the funnel as water flowed down, relieving the pressure in both jars.

3d. If the raised jar is held even higher, it finally runs out of water. Left in place, this outflow stops before the jar is fully drained. This happens when internal pressure (common to both jars) is no longer sufficient to lift water from its current level in the top jar to its outflow in the funnel. As this increasing height approaches the decreasing height of the water in the funnel (a measure of the overall pressure), the water slows to a trickle and finally stops.

Materials

- A 2-hole and 3-hole lid with rings that fit two jars of equal size.
- Two 50 cm tubes
- A funnel that reaches to the bottom of the jar. Extend short stems with tubing, if necessary.
- A medium-sized can.
- A clothespin.
- Clay.
- Petroleum jelly.
- A paper towel.

notes 18

(TO) apply Bernoulli's principle of low-pressure fluid streams to simple demonstrations involving a Ping-Pong ball.

BERNOULLI'S PRINCIPLE ○   Pressure ( )

1. The 18th century Swiss scientist, Daniel Bernoulli, noticed that moving air (or any other fluid) has lower internal pressure than when it is still. Hold a sheet of paper to your mouth and blow across it to observe this effect. Why does the paper rise?

2. Solve each Ping-Pong puzzle using Bernoulli's principle. Draw a diagram to illustrate each solution.

a. Touch the ball to a stream of tap water. Which way does it tend to move?

b. Blow straight down, across the mouth of the paper tube. Will the ball roll uphill?

c. Balance the ball on the end of a tube, then blow hard. Will it fall?

© 1992 by TOPS Learning Systems

Answers / Notes

1. According to Bernoulli's principle, the moving air on the top side of the paper has lower pressure than the stationary air underneath. Unequalized pressures on each side, therefore, press the paper upward.

2a. The ball moves into the lower pressure water stream, and is held there, by the higher pressure stationary air pressing in from behind. *(For brevity, some direction in this task card is carried solely by the illustrations. Taping string to the ball, for example, is implied rather than explicitly stated.)*

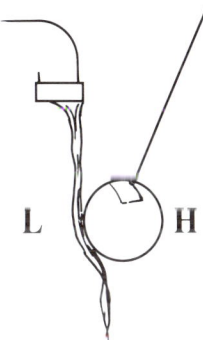

2b. The ball accelerates up the tube and out the other end, pushed from behind by the higher pressure of still air into the relatively lower pressure of moving air. *(Care must be taken to direct the air stream straight down, positioning the mouth directly above the tube. Blowing* into *rather than* past *the end of the tube, will move the ball backward rather than forward.)*

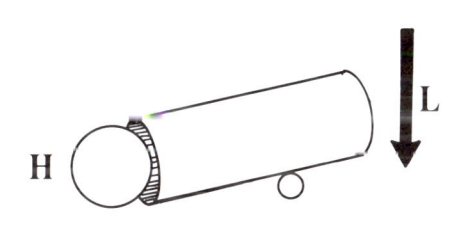

2c. Blow a hard as you like; the ball remains centered within the low pressure air stream, surrounded on all sides, and held in place, by a higher pressure stationary air mass.

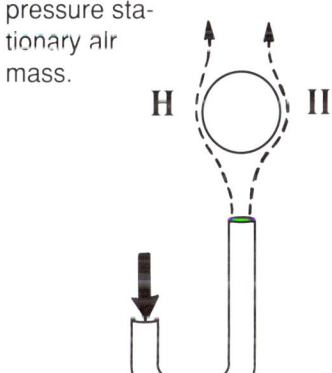

Materials
☐ A Ping-Pong ball.
☐ String.
☐ Masking tape.
☐ A faucet or pitcher.
☐ The cardboard tube from an empty toilet tissue roll.
☐ The 50 cm tube.
☐ The sanitary straw mouthpiece.

notes 19

(TO) measure the low pressure effects of moving air with a manometer, relating the speed of the airstream to the magnitude of the pressure changes. To construct an atomizer.

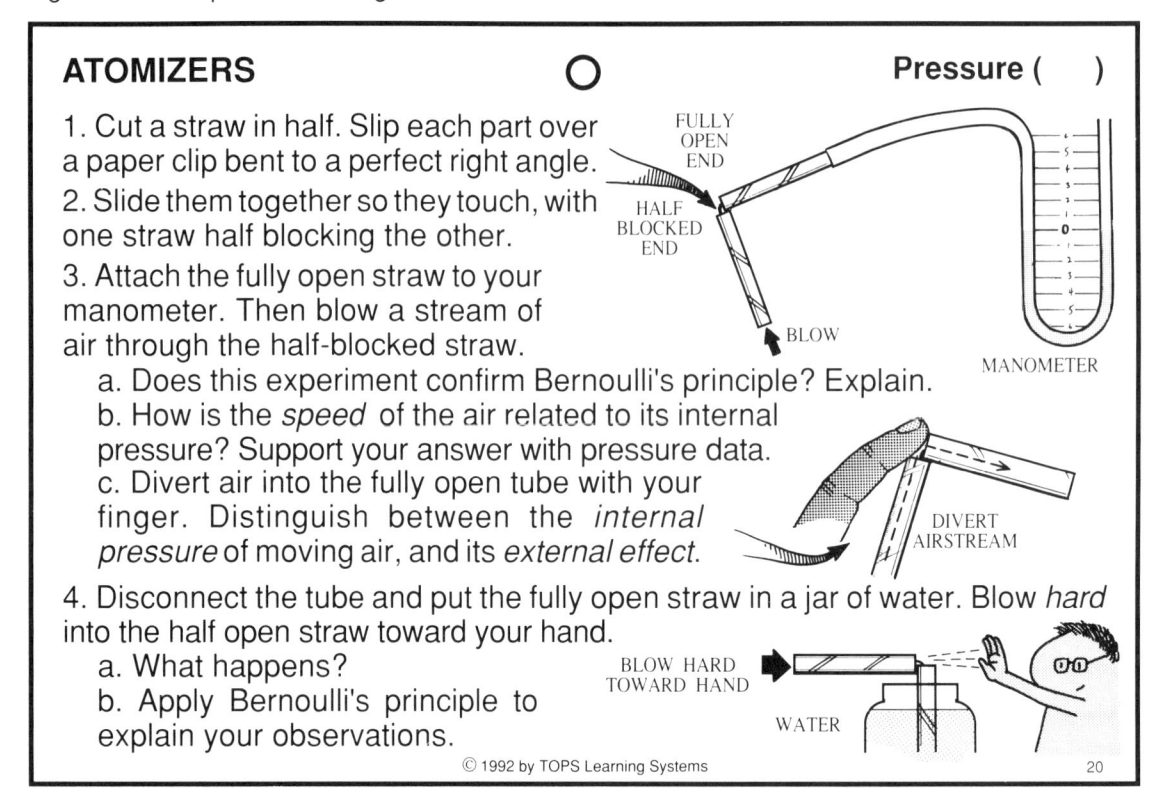

ATOMIGERS ◯   Pressure ( )

1. Cut a straw in half. Slip each part over a paper clip bent to a perfect right angle.
2. Slide them together so they touch, with one straw half blocking the other.
3. Attach the fully open straw to your manometer. Then blow a stream of air through the half-blocked straw.
    a. Does this experiment confirm Bernoulli's principle? Explain.
    b. How is the *speed* of the air related to its internal pressure? Support your answer with pressure data.
    c. Divert air into the fully open tube with your finger. Distinguish between the *internal pressure* of moving air, and its *external effect*.
4. Disconnect the tube and put the fully open straw in a jar of water. Blow *hard* into the half open straw toward your hand.
    a. What happens?
    b. Apply Bernoulli's principle to explain your observations.

© 1992 by TOPS Learning Systems

Answers / Notes

2. *The narrow end of the paper clip may need to be spread somewhat to firmly hold its half of the straw in place.*

3a. Yes. Water rises on the left side of the U and drops to the right, confirming the low pressure effect.

3b. As the speed of the airstream increases, the manometer registers decreasing pressure. A gentle air stream, for example, barely supports a perceptible difference in water levels. Blowing as hard as possible, however, evacuates the straw to as much as –6 cm of water.

3c. Diverting air *through* the tube, rather than *across* its end, raises the pressure in the manometer rather than lowering it. While an air stream has *internal* low pressure, it can still exert *external* high pressure on the manometer or any other object that blocks its path.

4a. Water flows up the straw and sprays against the hand. *(One must blow extremely hard to raise water up through the full length of the half-straw, a height of perhaps 10 cm. If the jar is filled near the brim, however, the straw can be dipped much deeper into the water, reducing pressure requirements dramatically.)*

4b. Internal low pressure in the air stream, directed across the mouth of the straw, allows higher atmospheric pressure to push water up to the top of the straw. At this point, this same air stream blows the water apart with high external pressure, into tiny droplets that spray against the hand.

Materials
☐ Scissors.
☐ A straw.
☐ A paper clip.
☐ The manometer.
☐ A jar.

(TO) construct an airfoil and observe how it flies. To account for its lift by applying Bernoulli's principle.

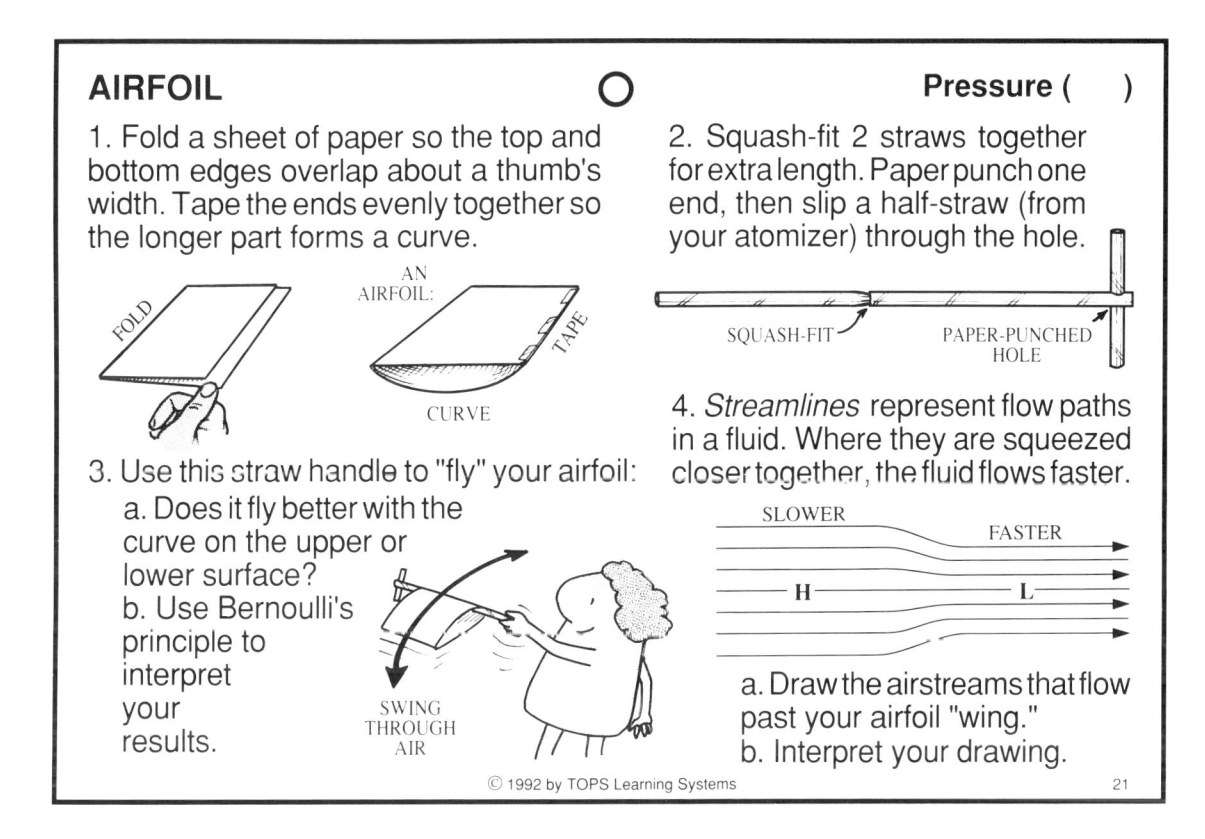

AIRFOIL   ◯   Pressure ( )

1. Fold a sheet of paper so the top and bottom edges overlap about a thumb's width. Tape the ends evenly together so the longer part forms a curve.

2. Squash-fit 2 straws together for extra length. Paper punch one end, then slip a half-straw (from your atomizer) through the hole.

3. Use this straw handle to "fly" your airfoil:
   a. Does it fly better with the curve on the upper or lower surface?
   b. Use Bernoulli's principle to interpret your results.

4. *Streamlines* represent flow paths in a fluid. Where they are squeezed closer together, the fluid flows faster.

   a. Draw the airstreams that flow past your airfoil "wing."
   b. Interpret your drawing.

© 1992 by TOPS Learning Systems

Answers / Notes

3a. The foil flies much better with the curve on the upper surface.

3b. Air travels a little faster across the curved surface of the foil than it does following the slightly shorter path across its flat side. This difference in air speed creates lower pressure on the curved side of the foil than on the flat side, creating a net lift when this curve points up.

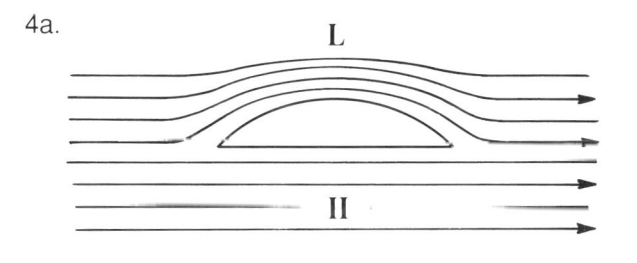

4a.

4b. The streamlines are forced closer together over the top, curved surface of the foil than across its bottom. This implies a faster flow over the top, hence a lower pressure, hence a net lift from higher pressure underneath.

Materials

☐ A sheet of paper.
☐ Masking tape or cellophane tape.
☐ Two straws plus the atomizer from the previous activity.
☐ A paper punch.

(TO) account for the curved flight of a spinning Ping-Pong ball using Bernoulli's principle.

SPIN AND CURVE ○ Pressure ( )

1. Cut a cardboard tube in half along its length. Lightly tape one of the halves to a book.

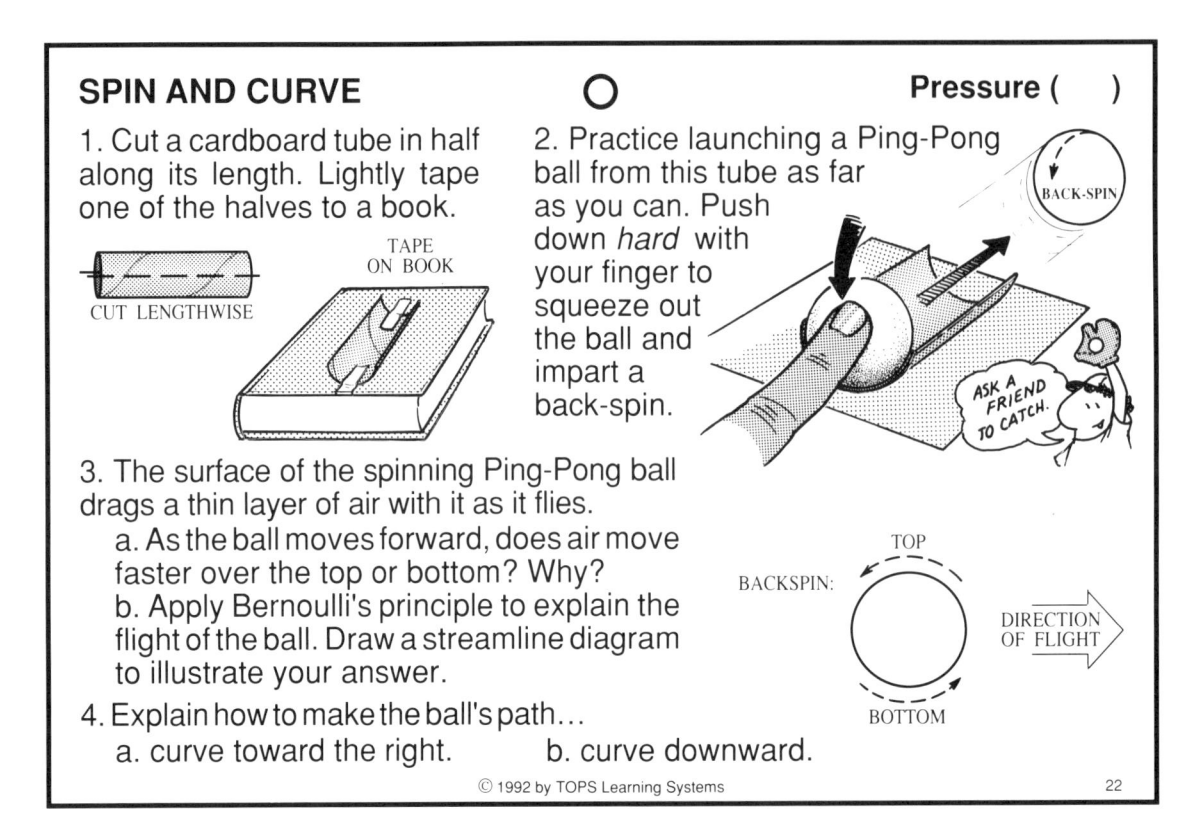

CUT LENGTHWISE — TAPE ON BOOK

2. Practice launching a Ping-Pong ball from this tube as far as you can. Push down *hard* with your finger to squeeze out the ball and impart a back-spin.

BACK-SPIN — ASK A FRIEND TO CATCH.

3. The surface of the spinning Ping-Pong ball drags a thin layer of air with it as it flies.
   a. As the ball moves forward, does air move faster over the top or bottom? Why?
   b. Apply Bernoulli's principle to explain the flight of the ball. Draw a streamline diagram to illustrate your answer.

4. Explain how to make the ball's path...
   a. curve toward the right.   b. curve downward.

BACKSPIN: TOP / BOTTOM — DIRECTION OF FLIGHT

© 1992 by TOPS Learning Systems

Answers / Notes

3a. As the ball moves forward, air flows faster over the top of the ball because it moves *with* this thin surface layer; air flows slower over the bottom because it moves *against* this layer.

3b. The ball curves upward because the faster air stream at the top of the ball has lower pressure than the slower air stream underneath. This pressure difference gives the ball lift, causing it to "float."

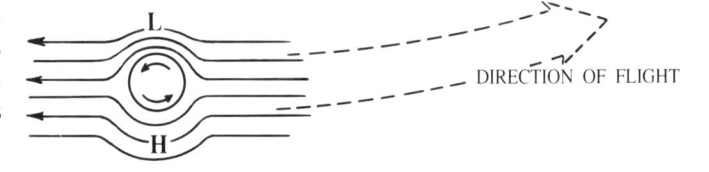

(L = low pressure above, H = high pressure below — DIRECTION OF FLIGHT)

4a. Hold the book vertically, with the tube on the right, to make the ball curve toward the right.

4b. Hold the launcher upside down to make the ball's flight curve downward.

Demonstration

You can put impressive spins on the Ping-Pong ball by launching it through a longer paper towel tube. Try this one in the gym or outside, where you have plenty of space.

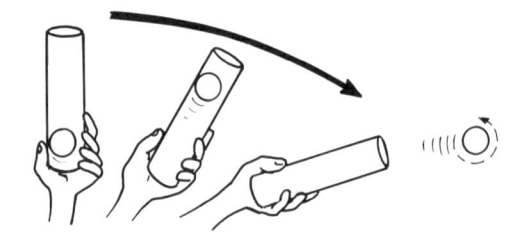

Materials

☐ The cardboard tube from a toilet tissue roll.
☐ Scissors.
☐ Masking tape.
☐ A book.
☐ A Ping-Pong ball.

(TO) fill a test tube with steam. To observe how the atmosphere pushes water inside to fill the vacuum created as the steam condenses.

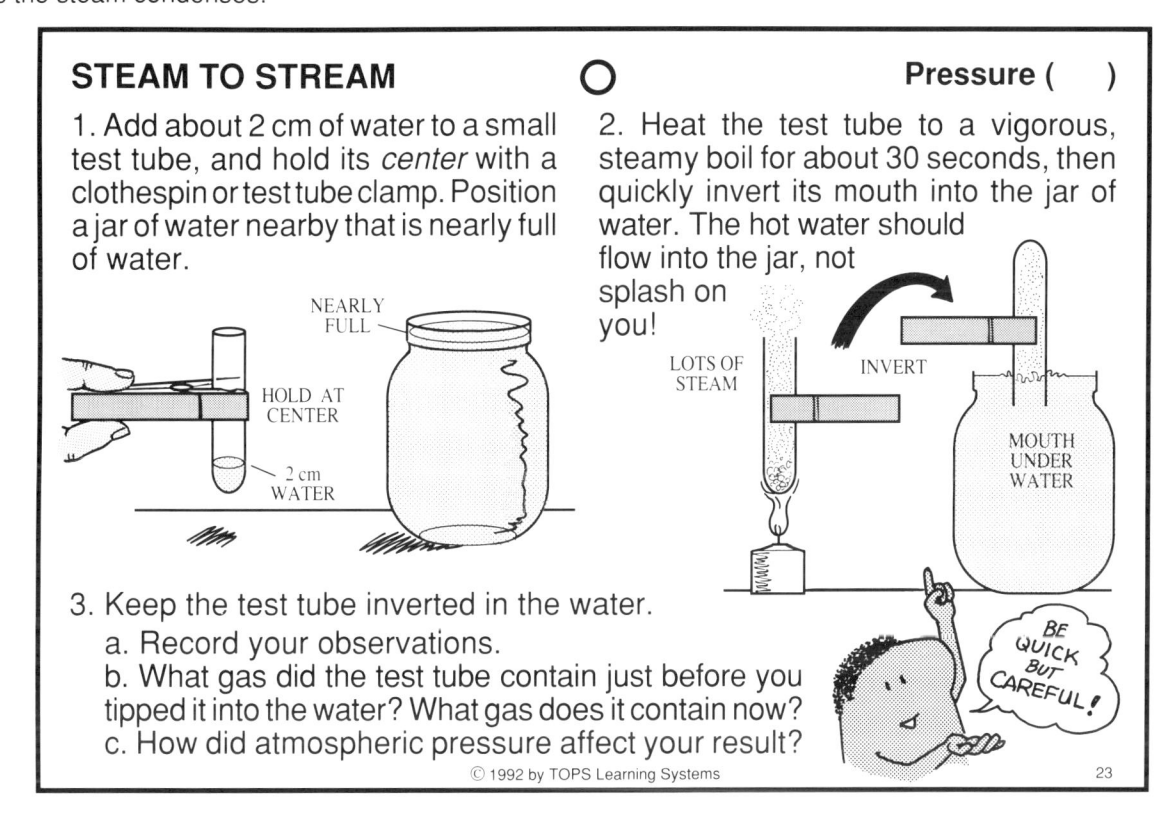

STEAM TO STREAM ◯ Pressure ( )

1. Add about 2 cm of water to a small test tube, and hold its *center* with a clothespin or test tube clamp. Position a jar of water nearby that is nearly full of water.

2. Heat the test tube to a vigorous, steamy boil for about 30 seconds, then quickly invert its mouth into the jar of water. The hot water should flow into the jar, not splash on you!

3. Keep the test tube inverted in the water.
   a. Record your observations.
   b. What gas did the test tube contain just before you tipped it into the water? What gas does it contain now?
   c. How did atmospheric pressure affect your result?

© 1992 by TOPS Learning Systems

Answers / Notes

3a. Water slowly rises inside the test tube, nearly to its top. *(This happens more rapidly if you cool the inverted tube with additional water. An eyedropper is convenient to use for this purpose.)*

3b. The test tube contained mostly water vapor (steam) after the water boiled vigorously inside. Now it contains a small amount of air. *(If air in the test tube was displaced by a good quantity of steam, what remains may be no larger than a bubble.)*

3c. As the steam cools and condenses, it takes up much less space, creating low pressure inside the test tube. Atmospheric pressure, acting in all directions, pushes additional water into the tube to fill the void.

Materials

- A test tube. Use the smallest size you have.
- A clothespin or test tube holder.
- A jar of water.
- A Bunsen burner, alcohol lamp or candle.
- Matches.
- An eyedropper (optional).

(TO) create a near vacuum in a test tube. To break its clay seal under water and watch the atmosphere push water into the void.

A PERFECT VACUUM?   Pressure ( )

1. Roll clay into an egg-shaped cap, so it rests on the mouth of a test tube like this:

2. Heat about 2 cm of water in your *open* test tube to a steamy boil for about 30 seconds, holding it at the top. Remove it from the flame while pressing in the clay cap *at the same time*, taking care not to burn your fingers on the steam.

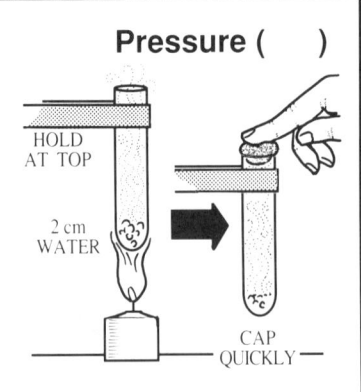

3. Allow your sealed test tube to cool to room temperature.
   a. Does atmospheric pressure now affect your test tube in any visible way?
   b. A *perfect vacuum* is empty space that contains no matter at all. Do you think your test tube now contains a perfect vacuum? Explain.

4. Predict what will happen if you break the clay seal under water. Give reasons for your answer.
   a. Test your prediction.
   b. Does your result indicate that you achieved a *perfect* vacuum? Explain.

© 1992 by TOPS Learning Systems

Answers / Notes

2. *Pressing on the cap and removing the test tube from the flame must happen simultaneously. If it remains over the flame while this cap is applied, the clay will rapidly melt into the tube. If it is applied too late, the vacuum will be compromised.*

3a. If the clay cap has properly sealed the test tube, the atmosphere will press it deeply into the mouth of the tube.

3b. The vacuum is not likely perfect. Some air that wasn't entirely purged by the steam may be left behind, plus a little water vapor.

4. The clay seal is now strong enough to resist the considerable pressure of Earth's atmosphere. Break this seal under water, and this same atmosphere will push water inside to immediately fill the vacuum.

4a. Students should comment on the accuracy of their prediction. *(The sudden rush of water is quite dramatic.)*

4b. No. A perfect vacuum was not achieved. A small bubble of air remained inside the tube. *(Remembering that this small air bubble once occupied the entire test tube save the space occupied by water, the rarity of the atmosphere is still impressive.)*

Extension

Describe the sound of splashing water when you shake an evacuated test tube, as compared to shaking a control that is identical in every respect but not evacuated.

Materials

☐ Oil-based modeling clay.
☐ A test tube. Use the smallest size you have.
☐ A clothespin or test tube holder.
☐ A Bunsen burner, alcohol lamp or candle.
☐ Matches.
☐ A jar of water.

(TO) calculate that maximum length that a test tube could reach and still have all its water supported by atmospheric pressure.

A VERY TALL TEST TUBE   Pressure ( )

1. Press a paper cap over the mouth of a test tube of water, and invert it over a tub. The atmosphere holds this water in with a pressure of roughly 10 N/cm^2. Does water press this hard from the inside? Explain.

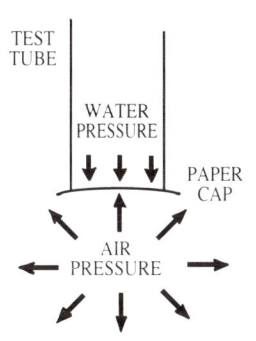

2. Empty and dry your tube. Trim a wedge of paper to fit the inside diameter. Use this to estimate its cross-sectional area in cm^2.

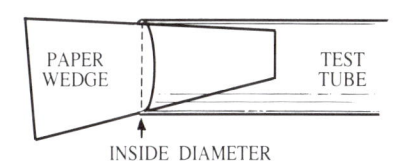

3. You will now calculate the maximum height a test tube full of water can reach, and still have all its water supported by atmospheric pressure.
   a. If 1 ml of water weighs about .01 Newton, use a graduated cylinder to estimate the total weight of water in your full tube.
   b. Calculate the water's pressure at the mouth of your inverted tube. How many times stronger is the atmospheric pressure that holds it up?
   c. Measure the height of your test tube in centimeters. How much higher could this tube of water reach before atmospheric pressure is overcome and the water falls out?

© 1992 by TOPS Learning Systems   25

Answers / Notes

1. No. Water presses the other side of the paper disk with a pressure that is less than 10 N/cm^2. Otherwise it would push the atmosphere out of the way and fall out of the tube.

2. Calculations in this activity derive from the particular test tube you are using. Our 29 ml-capacity, 15 cm-long tube has an inside diameter of 1.6 cm, yielding a cross-sectional area of 2.0 cm^2.

3a. weight of water in test tube = 29 ml × $\frac{.01 \text{ N}}{\text{ml}}$ = .29 N.

3b. water pressure at mouth = $\frac{F}{A}$ = $\frac{.29 \text{ N}}{2.0 \text{ cm}^2}$ = .145 N/cm^2

   number of times atmosphere is stronger = $\frac{10 \text{ N/cm}^2}{.145 \text{ N/cm}^2}$ = 69 times

3c. maximum height of test tube = 15 cm × 69 = 1035 cm.

A very clever student may recognize that the information provided in 3a is all he or she really needs to know: Imagine each 1 ml volume of water shaped into a perfect cube measuring 1 cm on a side. Then 1000 of these cubes stacked into a neat column would reach 10 meters high and exert a pressure of 1000 × .01 Newtons (10 N/cm^2) against the bottom.

Discussion

Would the calculations above work for a bottle instead of a test tube? (No. Most of the water in an inverted bottle is supported by its sloping glass sides, not the paper disk. Only the circular column of water directly over the mouth of the bottle is supported by air. This is why height, not volume, is the important consideration when measuring atmospheric pressure.)

Materials

☐ Scissors.
☐ A test tube. Use the largest size you have on hand.
☐ A tub or equivalent container.
☐ A paper towel.
☐ A metric ruler.
☐ The Area Estimator (for square centimeters).
☐ A graduated cylinder.
☐ A calculator (optional).

(**TO**) experimentally calculate atmospheric pressure in N/cm^2.

MEASURE THE PRESSURE ○   Pressure ( )

1. The right amount of water in a plastic milk jug, when pulling straight down on the plunger of a sealed plastic syringe, will *slowly* open a vacuum in its chamber.
   a. Identify two kinds of forces overcome by this water jug.
   b. Experiment to find the volume of water needed to overcome these combined forces.

2. Find the volume of water needed to overcome friction *alone*; atmospheric pressure *alone*. Show your work.

3. Calculate atmospheric pressure:
   a. Trim a wedge of paper to measure the inside diameter of your syringe. Use this to estimate its cross-sectional area in cm^2.
   b. Knowing that water weighs about .01 N/ml, find the total force distributed over this much area.
   c. Divide to find the pressure. How close did you come to the accepted rough value of 10 N/cm^2?

© 1992 by TOPS Learning Systems   26

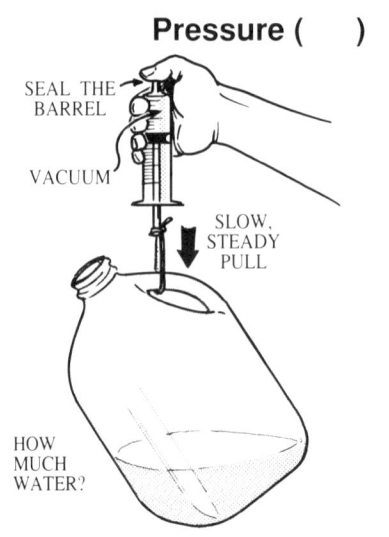

Answers / Notes

1a. The weight of water in the jug overcomes two forces: the atmosphere pushing the plunger in, and friction holding the plunger inside its barrel.

1b. Data is dependent on the cross-sectional area of each particular syringe and its unique internal friction. Ours opened very slowly with 790 ml of water inside the milk jug.

2. In our particular syringe, the volume of water needed to overcome friction alone was 160 ml. This was found by repeating the procedure in 1b above, but with one important difference: leaving its end open to the atmosphere. *(Sticky syringes may require a nudge to get them started. Once underway they should open slowly, at about the same speed as when the end of the plunger was blocked to form a vacuum.)*

       overcomes friction and air pressure: jug + 790 ml water
     − overcomes friction alone: jug + 160 ml water
       overcomes air pressure alone: 630 ml water

3a-3c.   estimated cross-sectional area of syringe = .6 cm^2

force distributed over this area = 630 ml × $\frac{.01 \text{ N}}{\text{ml}}$ = 6.3 N

pressure needed to just push back the atmosphere = $\frac{F}{A}$ = $\frac{6.3 \text{ N}}{.6 \text{ cm}^2}$ = 10.5 N/cm^2

% error = $\frac{\text{difference}}{\text{accepted value}}$ × 100 = $\frac{.5 \text{ N/cm}^2}{10 \text{ N/cm}^2}$ × 100 = 5%

Materials
☐ A small syringe with about a 3 cc capacity.
☐ String.
☐ A plastic gallon milk jug with a handle. Smaller capacity jugs will also serve.
☐ A sink or tub.
☐ Scissors.
☐ The Area Estimator (for square centimeters).
☐ A calculator (optional).

(TO) design and build a vacuum pump. To understand how one-way valves and atmospheric pressure act to lift water.

VACUUM PUMP   **Pressure ( )**

1. Take the bulb off an eyedropper. Fit a piece of tubing, as long as the barrel, over the glass rim.

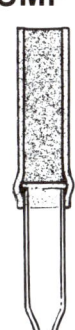

TUBING
GLASS BARREL

2. Drop a BB into its nose. Slip the nose of a second eyedropper into the tube, then draw water up by squeezing the bulb.
   a. What can you discover?
   b. Would this happen without the BB? Without atmospheric pressure? Explain.

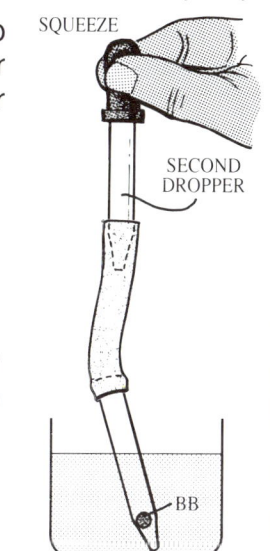

SQUEEZE
SECOND DROPPER
BB

3. Replace the bulb on your second dropper with a longer tube. Use this to build a vacuum pump that lifts water from a lower jar to a higher jar resting on a can.
   a. Diagram your solution.
   b. Explain how your vacuum pump works.
   c. What is the maximum height that a vacuum pump (even a high-tech one) can lift water? Why?
   d. Can you think of a way to pump water higher than this limitation?
   e. Take your pump apart. Put the bulbs back on the dropper barrels.

© 1992 by TOPS Learning Systems   27

Answers / Notes

2a. Water rises into the dropper barrel but can't run back out. Additional squeezing draws up more water until it reaches the top dropper bulb and squirts out from under its seal.

2b. Both the BB and atmospheric pressure are needed to sustain this pumping action. The BB acts as a one-way valve, lifting as water flows in, then blocking the intake opening to prevent back flow. Atmospheric pressure acts to equalize the inside pressure, pushing water up the barrel whenever the squeezed bulb is relaxed.

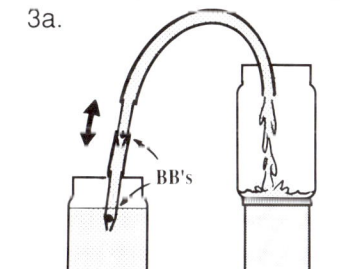

3a.

BB's

3b. To operate this pump, move the top barrel down and up inside the short tube. With each down stroke, water flows past the upper BB into the top barrel, pushed by higher pressure from below. During the up stroke, water flows past the lower BB into the bottom barrel, pushed by outside atmospheric pressure.

3c. A vacuum pump cannot draw up water past about 10.3 meters. At this height, there is a perfect vacuum above the water that can't be further evacuated.

3d. Exert positive pressure on the water, as strong as you like, to push the water uphill as far as you want. This is similar to squeezing the water bag in activity 8. Or use a series of vacuum pumps that raise water from one reservoir to another in stair-step jumps of less than 10.3 meters.

Extension

Design a hand-operated vacuum pump to lift water from a well. Expert factory engineers are standing by to supply you with all fittings, tubes and valves in any shape and size that you specify.

Materials

☐ Two BB's. Standard BB shot has a diameter of about 5/32 inch.
☐ Two eyedroppers with straight barrels and tapered noses. Make sure the BB's roll freely in the barrel but lodge in the nose. If your droppers are too narrow, substitute glass tubing with a wider diameter. Stretch out the glass in a hot flame. Cool and divide to form tapered ends.
☐ A short (8 cm) piece of 1/4 inch tubing. If you plan to teach this module again, cut this from new stock to preserve your 3 longer standards. Stretch open an end with needle-nose pliers so the snout of the top eyedropper easily slides in and out.
☐ The 50 cm tube.
☐ Two jars and a tin can.

(TO) fill a jar with just enough water to simulate a pressure of 1/10 atmosphere. To develop a standard of comparison to use in the next activity.

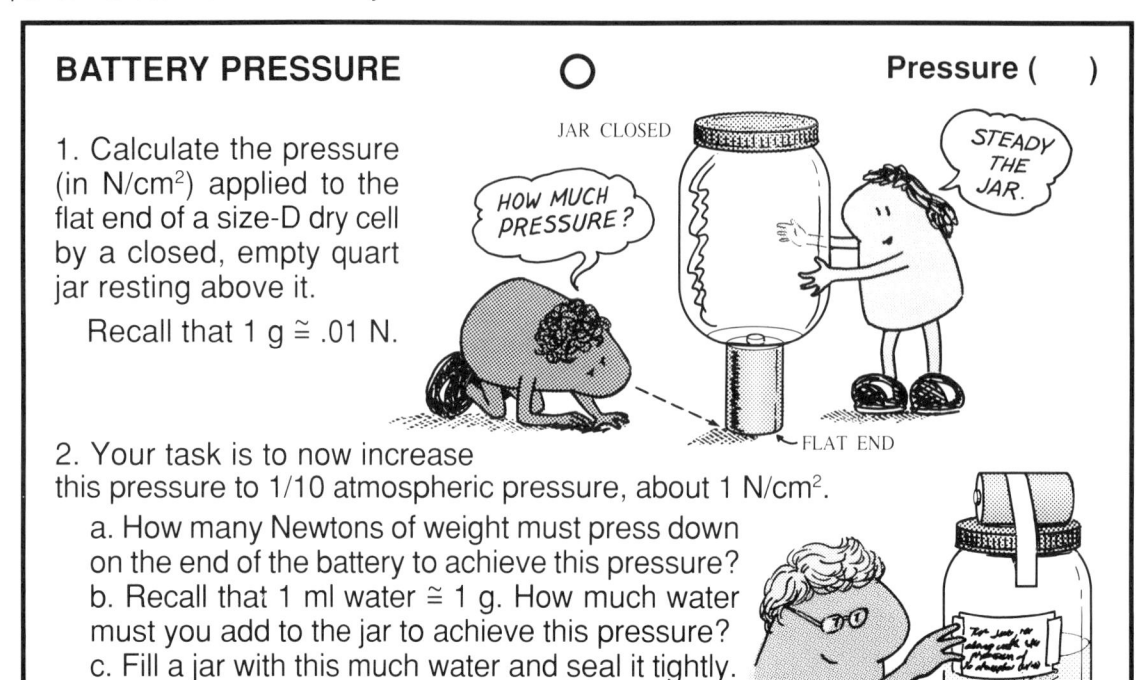

BATTERY PRESSURE ◯   Pressure (   )

1. Calculate the pressure (in N/cm^2) applied to the flat end of a size-D dry cell by a closed, empty quart jar resting above it.

Recall that 1 g ≅ .01 N.

2. Your task is to now increase this pressure to 1/10 atmospheric pressure, about 1 N/cm^2.
  a. How many Newtons of weight must press down on the end of the battery to achieve this pressure?
  b. Recall that 1 ml water ≅ 1 g. How much water must you add to the jar to achieve this pressure?
  c. Fill a jar with this much water and seal it tightly.
  d. Label the jar with an appropriate title and tape the battery to the top.

© 1992 by TOPS Learning Systems   28

Answers / Notes

1. These sample calculations are based on a 386 g jar and a 101 g size-D battery:

mass of jar + battery = 487 g

weight of jar + battery = 487 g × $\frac{.01 \text{ N}}{1 \text{ g}}$ = 4.87 N

area of flat end of battery = 9 cm^2

pressure = $\frac{4.87 \text{ N}}{9 \text{ cm}^2}$ = .54 N/cm^2

2a. $\frac{1 \text{ N}}{\text{cm}^2}$ × 9 cm^2 = 9 N

2b.
target weight = 9.00 N
less weight of jar + battery = 4.87 N
needed water = 5.13 N = 513 ml

2d. Sample label:

> This jar,
> when resting on its battery,
> exerts a pressure
> of 1/10 atmosphere
> (1 N/cm^2)

Materials

☐ A size-D battery, dead or alive.
☐ A quart jar with lid and ring.
☐ A jar for pouring water.
☐ The Area Estimator (for sq cm).
☐ A large capacity scale (optional). Or find the mass of jars and batteries in advance, and label them for student use.
☐ A graduated cylinder.
☐ A calculator (optional).

(TO) estimate the maximum air pressure that one can exert with the lungs.

MAXIMUM LUNG PRESSURE? ○   Pressure ( )

1. Gather the mouth of a sandwich bag around the end of a tube. Seal with at least 10 turns of string covered with tape.
2. Cut scratch paper in half the short way. Roll it evenly around a size-D battery and secure with tape.
3. Punch a hole, just above the dry cell, with a nail. Thread your tube through this hole so the bag fits inside.
4. Adjust the bag so it puffs out the top only about 2 cm when you blow into the tube.

 a. Use this small "air bag" and your labeled jar with battery from the previous activity to estimate your maximum lung pressure.
 b. Why is it important to start with the bag *entirely* inside the tube?

© 1992 by TOPS Learning Systems

Answers / Notes

4a. Your students will discover that their maximum lung pressure is somewhere near 1/10 atmospheric pressure, or 1 N/cm². Those who find it to be more or less than this can report this qualitatively, or adjust the volume of water in the jar to obtain a quantitative result:

$$\text{pressure of jar} = \frac{1\text{ N}}{\text{cm}^2} = \frac{9\text{ N}}{9\text{ cm}^2} = \frac{900\text{ ml}}{9\text{ cm}^2}$$

Thus adding or subtracting water from the jar in 9 ml increments changes the pressure at the end of the battery in .01 N increments.

4b. The bag must be confined inside the tube to restrict its surface area to 9 cm², the same size as the end of the battery. If allowed to mushroom out beyond these confines, then your lung pressure acts over a larger surface area, allowing the jar to be lifted with pressures less than 1 N/cm².

 The jar, with battery taped on top, can rest directly on the paper tube as illustrated. Or the battery itself can be shallowly inserted into the top of the tube, bump side down, with the jar resting upon the flat end. This latter method insures that the rising surface of the bag underneath remains confined to 9 cm². The former method is preferred, at least initially, because the jar is more stable.

Materials

☐ A plastic sandwich bag.
☐ The 50 cm tube.
☐ String.
☐ Masking tape.
☐ Scissors.
☐ A sharp nail. A dull nail will serve if a starting hole is first drilled with a straight pin.
☐ The labeled quart jar with battery from the previous experiment.
☐ Another size-D battery, dead or alive.
☐ A jar for pouring water.
☐ The sanitary straw mouthpiece.

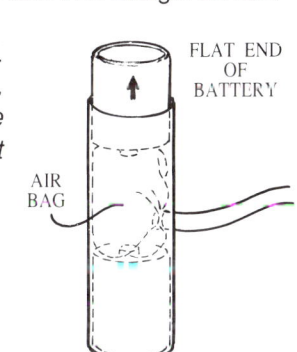

(TO) calculate the maximum load you can lift by blowing air into a produce bag. To use body weight to confirm that your calculated force has the correct order of magnitude.

BIG LIFT　　　　　O　　　　　**Pressure ( )**

1. Take apart your air bag assembly from the last activity. Attach a larger produce bag to the end of the tube with at least 10 turns of string, as before.

2. Flatten the bag, smoothing it out to its maximum 2-dimensional size. Estimate its top (or bottom) surface area with two centimeter grids taped together. Recall how you did this in activity 2.

3. Recall your maximum lung pressure determined in the previous activity.
   a. Use this value to estimate the maximum weight, in Newtons, that you can lift with this bag.
   b. Convert your answer to pounds. (1 N = .22 lbs)
   c. The maximum force you can lift with this bag decreases as you continue to blow air into it. Explain why.

4. Test your prediction using body weight. Explain what you did.

© 1992 by TOPS Learning Systems

Answers / Notes

2. Our particular produce bag had a surface area of 520 cm². *As before, students should "x-out" squares around the perimeter of the tracing that have areas of less than 1/2 square, then count all that remain in a systematic fashion. To avoid losing count, they might label every hundredth square.*

3. These calculations are based on a maximum lung pressure of 1 N/cm².

3a. $\frac{1 \text{ N}}{\text{cm}^2} \times 520 \text{ cm}^2 = 520 \text{ N}$　　　　3b. $520 \text{ N} \times \frac{.22 \text{ lbs}}{\text{N}} = 114 \text{ lbs}$

3c. With no air inside, the entire top surface of the bag presses against the load. But as you fill the bag with air, less and less of its surface area maintains contact. In other words, as the height of the load increases, less of the bag's surface area is devoted to pushing *up*, while more is devoted to pushing *out* against the sides.

4. Students should attempt to lift their own weight, either by leaning on a clipboard (or equivalent) with their hands, or by sitting on it. By partially supporting themselves with hands or feet, they can roughly approximate the weight calculated in 3b. Or they can attempt to lift a classmate, either sitting or standing.

Demonstration

Overturn a table on the floor. Position perhaps 8 bags under the outside edge. Estimate the force that these 8 bags can apply to a teacher standing on the table. (This will add up to nearly 1/2 ton!) Finally, confirm that you weigh much less than this.

Materials

- ☐ The tube with connected sandwich bag from the previous activity.
- ☐ A produce bag.
- ☐ String and scissors.
- ☐ Masking tape.
- ☐ Two copies of the photocopied centimeter grid.
- ☐ The sanitary straw mouthpiece.
- ☐ A long strong clipboard, thick telephone book, or square of plywood.

(TO) observe how changes in temperature and volume affect pressure. To develop equations that relate these variables.

THREE VARIABLES   Pressure ( )

1. Connect your manometer to a jar with a 1-hole lid. Seal it airtight with grease.

2. Warm the jar with your hands. Cool it with a paper towel dampened with rubbing alcohol.

3. Squeeze and relax the tube between the jar and manometer. This compresses and expands the volume of air inside the closed system.

a. Complete this table.

TEMP	PRESSURE
INCREASE	
DECREASE	

a. Complete this table.

VOLUME	PRESSURE
DECREASE	
INCREASE	

b. Consider these equations:

$$P = kT, \quad P = k/T \quad \leftarrow \text{(k is any constant number)} \rightarrow \quad P = kV, \quad P = k/V$$

Which one best summarizes your observations? Explain.

Which one best summarizes your observations? Explain.

4. Consider these equations: $PT = kV$, $PV = kT$, $VT = kP$. Which one best summarizes all observations in this activity? Explain your reasoning.

© 1992 by TOPS Learning Systems

Answers / Notes

2a.

TEMP	PRESSURE
INCREASE	INCREASE
DECREASE	DECREASE

2b. The equation $P = kT$ best expresses this relationship. As T increases [0, 1, 2, 3,...], P increases as well [k(0), k(1), k(2), k(3),...].

3a.

VOLUME	PRESSURE
DECREASE	INCREASE
INCREASE	DECREASE

3b. The equation $P = k/V$ best expresses this relationship. As V increases [1, 2, 3, 4,...], P decreases [k/1, k/2, k/3, k/4...].

4. The equation $PV = kT$ fits all observations. It implies that pressure is proportional to temperature (both rise and fall together); it implies that pressure is inversely proportional to volume (one raises as the other falls). Neither of the other two equations satisfy both trends.

Materials

☐ The manometer.
☐ A canning jar with a 1-hole lid and ring.
☐ Petroleum jelly.
☐ Rubbing alcohol (optional). Water will produce a slower, yet observable, pressure drop.
☐ A paper towel.
☐ An eye dropper.

(TO) model how an aneroid barometer works. To build an instrument that measures atmospheric pressure.

ANEROID BAROMETER   Pressure ( )

1. Tightly cover the top of a small container with plastic wrap, then seal it airtight with a rubber band. Fix the wide end of a toothpick to the center with drops of melted wax from a burning candle.

2. After the wax hardens, carefully place the entire assembly in the bottom of a jar. Seal with your 1-hole lid and insert a rubber tube.

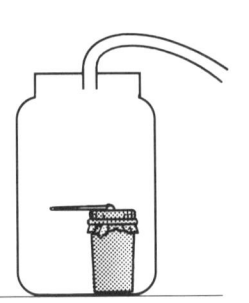

3. A *barometer* measures changes in atmospheric pressure. An *aneroid* barometer does this without liquid.
   a. How do the plastic wrap and toothpick respond as you change the air pressure inside the jar?
   b. Have you made an aneroid barometer? Explain.

4. This device is probably not sensitive enough to measure the high pressure of a sunny day, or the low pressure of a rainy day.
   a. Design and build a larger, more sensitive instrument. Use it to forecast changes in the weather.
   b. What *other* variable must be kept constant to accurately track changes in atmospheric pressure? Explain.

© 1992 by TOPS Learning Systems

Answers / Notes

3a. Blowing air into the jar (increasing its inside pressure) depresses the plastic wrap into its canister, thus raising the toothpick indicator. Similarly, sucking air out of the jar (lowering its inside pressure) bulges the plastic wrap above its canister, thus lowering the toothpick indicator.

3b. Yes, this is an aneroid barometer. It measures changes in air pressure without the presence of a liquid.

4a. Here is one design. The large capacity jug, its small mouth and long indicator straw all maximize sensitivity to small pressure changes. A rising needle suggests rising pressure with improving weather. A falling needle suggest falling pressure with deteriorating weather.

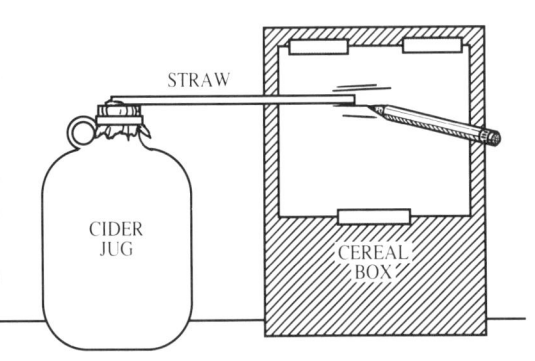

4b. To accurately measure changes in atmospheric pressure outside the jar, changes in air temperature inside the jar must be held constant. If not, then there is no way to distinguish to which variable the indicator needle is responding.

Materials

☐ A film canister or pill container that is short enough to fit lengthwise through the mouth of your canning jar.
☐ Plastic wrap.
☐ Scissors.
☐ Rubber bands.
☐ A flat toothpick. A short length of straw will also serve.
☐ A candle and matches.
☐ A canning jar with 1-hole lid and ring.
☐ The 50 cm tube.
☐ The sanitary straw mouthpiece.
☐ Materials to build a full-scale aneroid barometer: A large cider jug will give the best results. A straw, or even two squash-fitted together, will provide a good indicator. A cereal box with paper might serve to record needle fluctuations.

REPRODUCIBLE STUDENT TASK CARDS

☞ As you duplicate and distribute these task cards, **please observe our copyright restrictions** at the front of this book. Our basic rule is: **One book, one teacher.**

☞ TOPS is a small, not-for-profit educational corporation, dedicated to making great science accessible to students everywhere. Our only income is from the sale of these inexpensive modules. If you would like to help spread the word that TOPS is tops, please request multiple copies of our **free TOPS Ideas catalog** to pass on to other educators or student teachers. These offer a variety of sample lessons, plus an order form for your colleagues to purchase their own TOPS modules. Thanks!

Task Cards Options

Here are 3 management options to consider before you photocopy:

1. Consumable Worksheets: Copy 1 complete set of task card pages. Cut out each card and fix it to a separate sheet of boldly lined paper. Duplicate a class set of each worksheet master you have made, 1 per student. Direct students to follow the task card instructions at the top of each page, then respond to questions in the lined space underneath.

2. Nonconsumable Reference Booklets: Copy and collate the 2-up task card pages in sequence. Make perhaps half as many sets as the students who will use them. Staple each set in the upper left corner, both front and back to prevent the outside pages from working loose. Tell students that these task card booklets are for reference only. They should use them as they would any textbook, responding to questions on their own papers, returning them unmarked and in good shape at the end of the module.

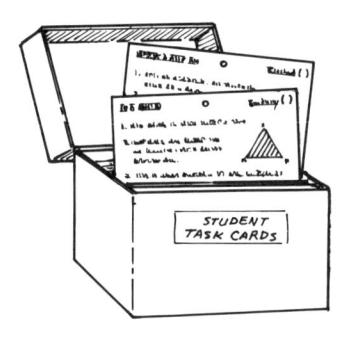

3. Nonconsumable Task Cards: Copy several sets of task card pages. Laminate them, if you wish, for extra durability, then cut out each card to display in your room. You might pin cards to bulletin boards; or punch out the holes and hang them from wall hooks (you can fashion hooks from paper clips and tape these to the wall); or fix cards to cereal boxes with paper fasteners, 4 to a box; or keep cards on designated reference tables. The important thing is to provide enough task card reference points about your classroom to avoid a jam of too many students at any one location. Two or 3 task card sets should accommodate everyone, since different students will use different cards at different times.

SQUEEZE PLAY   Pressure (   )

1. Roll a lump of clay into the size of a round Ping-Pong ball.

2. Sandwich it between 2 half pieces of index card, then squeeze it with the force of your own weight against a hard floor.

3. Use the Area Estimator (for Square Inches) to estimate the *area* (A) of your newly formed disk. Divide this into the *force* of your own weight (F) to find the *pressure* (P) that you applied.

$$P = \frac{F}{A}$$

4. Repeat steps 1-3 for marble- and pea-sized clay spheres. Save all three clay disks for step 5.

5. Relate the thickness of each disk to the pressures you have calculated.

6. You applied the same force to each lump of clay. Why, then, do the pressures change?

© 1992 by TOPS Learning Systems

PRESSURE PRINT   Pressure (   )

1. Outline the perimeter of your shoe on a Centimeter Grid.

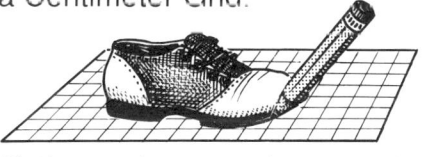

2. Estimate its area by counting centimeter squares. Count all squares greater than 1/2 as "one," all squares less than 1/2 as "zero."

3. Convert your weight from pounds to Newtons using this graph. What average pressure (in N/cm^2) do you exert when standing on 1 foot?

4. How does this pressure change when standing, with equal balance, on both feet? Explain your reasoning.

5. Earth's atmosphere exerts a pressure of about 10 N/cm^2 against the floor. Describe how you should stand to approximate this much pressure.

© 1992 by TOPS Learning Systems

PASCAL'S PRINCIPLE ◯ Pressure (   )

1. Wrap masking tape evenly around the end of a straw, so it can snugly fit into rubber tubing. Then remove the tubing.

2. Gather the mouth of a sandwich bag around the taped end of the straw. Firmly wrap with at least 10 turns of string to seal it airtight, then tape over the string.

3. Blow into the bag, while gently squeezing and relaxing it in your hand.
   a. Describe the pressure changes you feel in your hands and lungs.
   b. You are holding *fluid* in a *closed system*: What is this fluid? Describe the closed system.

4. Apply Pascal's principle to this experiment.

5. Lift a book off your table using lung pressure.
   a. Describe how you did this.
   b. How does air press to move the book up? Draw a diagram. (Label your straw with a masking tape tag and save it to use as a sanitary mouthpiece.)

© 1992 by TOPS Learning Systems

PRESS YOUR ADVANTAGE ◯ Pressure (   )

1. Fill a sandwich bag and a produce bag about 2/3 full of air. Attach them to your tube with string, as before, so the seal is airtight.

2. Squeeze air back and forth between the larger and smaller bags.
   a. Must you push with equal *force* to move the air between bags? Write your observations.
   b. Does the air in each bag press against the same surface *area*?
   c. Will squeezing one bag increase *pressure* in the other bag by an equal amount? Apply Pascal's principle.

3. Recall how pressure is defined. Do your observations in step 2 concerning F, A and P support this equation? Explain.

$$P = \frac{F}{A}$$

4. Use just 1 book to lift 2 books.
   a. Diagram how you did this.
   b. This machine gives you a force advantage. What is the disadvantage?

© 1992 by TOPS Learning Systems

cards 3-4

OCEAN OF AIR ◯ Pressure ( )

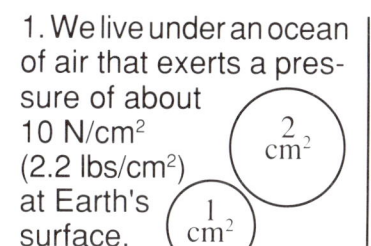

1. We live under an ocean of air that exerts a pressure of about 10 N/cm² (2.2 lbs/cm²) at Earth's surface.

   2 cm²
   1 cm²
   4 cm²

   a. How many Newtons of force are pressing on each of these circles right now? How many pounds?

   b. If so much force acts on just these circles, why does this whole paper feel so light?

2. Tie string to a paper clip taped to the center of scratch paper resting on your table. Now jerk up on the string to lift the paper as fast as possible.

   a. What happens?
   b. Repeat the experiment with the paper resting on a canning ring.
   c. What can you conclude?

3. Push a sandwich bag deep into a jar, then fold its top over the rim. Seal it airtight with at least 6 turns of string and hold the loose end.

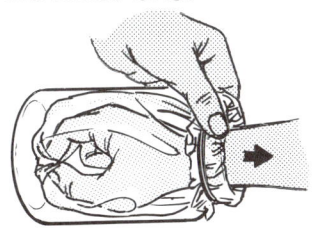

   a. Why can't you easily pull out the bag?
   b. Estimate the force (in both Newtons and pounds) that pushes in from outside the jar.

© 1992 by TOPS Learning Systems

SNAP AND POP ◯ Pressure ( )

1. Get a small syringe with no needle. Push the plunger fully in, then seal the other end with your finger. What happens if you pull the plunger…

   a. out until it separates from the barrel? Why?
   b. out halfway then let it go? Why?

2. Do you get the same results in step 1 if you leave the end of the barrel open? Why?

3. Consider two syringes with different diameters.

   a. If you sealed each one with your finger, would you expect to pull out each plunger using about the same amount of force? Make a prediction, giving reasons for your answer.
   b. Evaluate your prediction.

4. Use a syringe to show that Earth's atmosphere exerts pressure in *all* directions.

© 1992 by TOPS Learning Systems

cards 5-6

TOWERS OF WATER   O   Pressure ( )

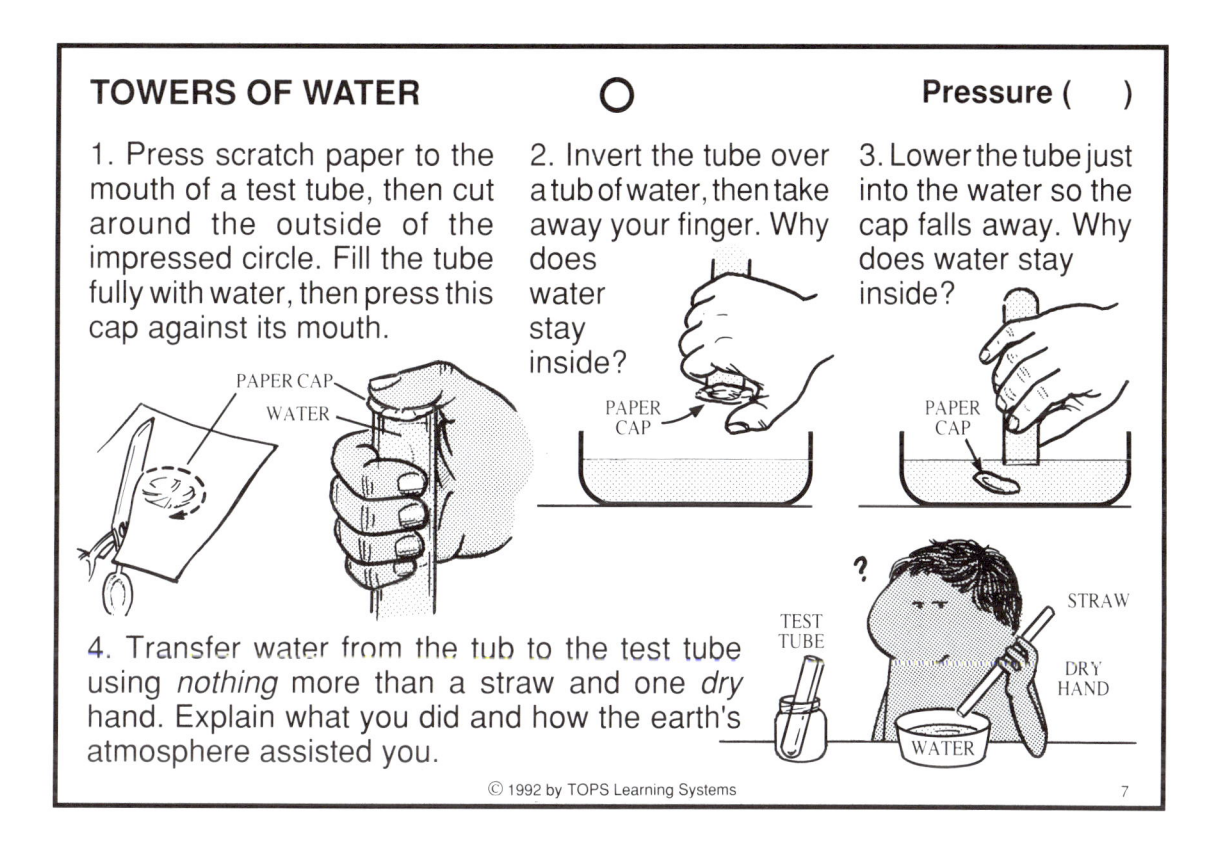

1. Press scratch paper to the mouth of a test tube, then cut around the outside of the impressed circle. Fill the tube fully with water, then press this cap against its mouth.

2. Invert the tube over a tub of water, then take away your finger. Why does water stay inside?

3. Lower the tube just into the water so the cap falls away. Why does water stay inside?

4. Transfer water from the tub to the test tube using *nothing* more than a straw and one *dry* hand. Explain what you did and how the earth's atmosphere assisted you.

© 1992 by TOPS Learning Systems

7

RISE AND FALL (1)   O   Pressure ( )

1. Reinforce the bottom of a plastic cup with crossed strips of masking tape. Gently drill a hole though its middle with a large, sharp nail.

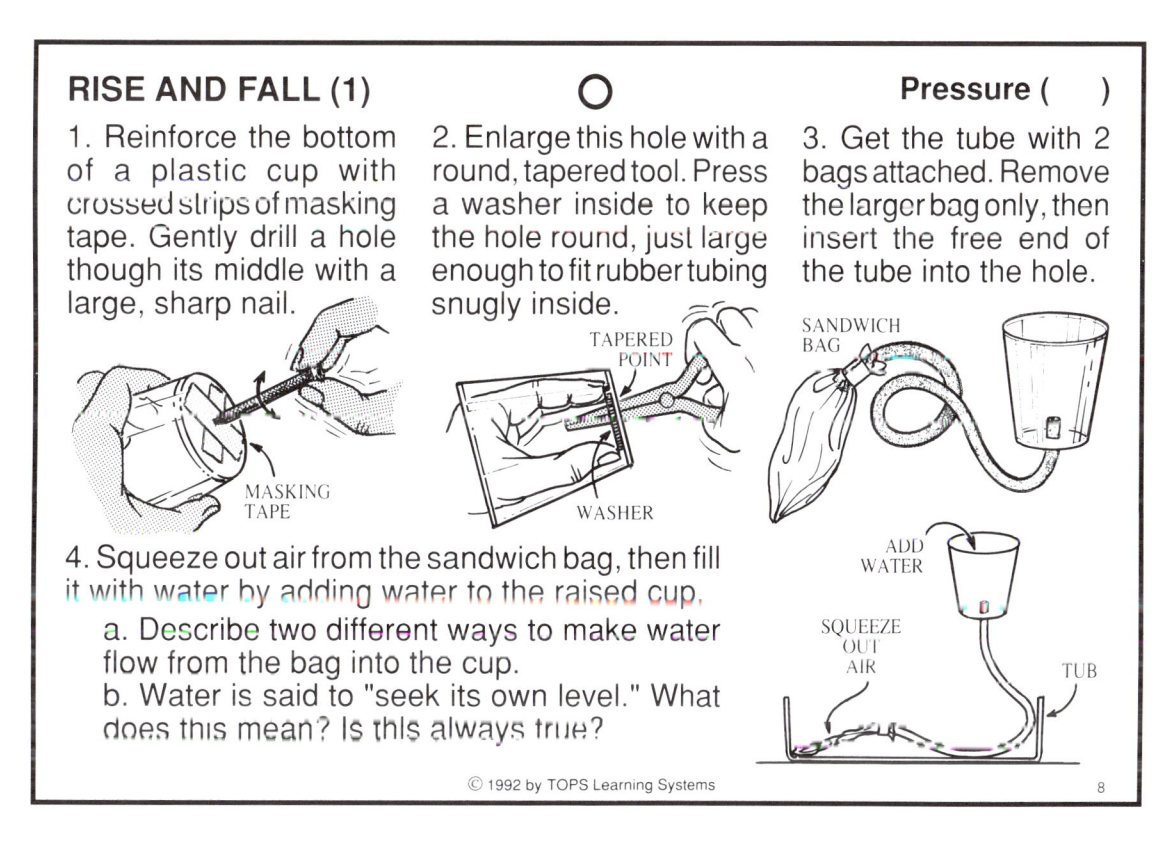

2. Enlarge this hole with a round, tapered tool. Press a washer inside to keep the hole round, just large enough to fit rubber tubing snugly inside.

3. Get the tube with 2 bags attached. Remove the larger bag only, then insert the free end of the tube into the hole.

4. Squeeze out air from the sandwich bag, then fill it with water by adding water to the raised cup.
    a. Describe two different ways to make water flow from the bag into the cup.
    b. Water is said to "seek its own level." What does this mean? Is this always true?

© 1992 by TOPS Learning Systems

8

cards 7-8

BREATHING MACHINE   Pressure (   )

1. Untie the sandwich bag from the tube. Pull the other end further through the cup.

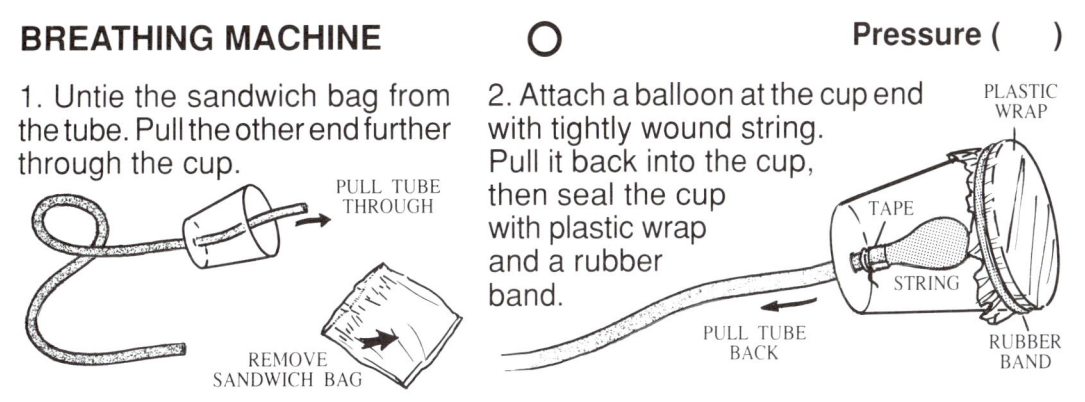

2. Attach a balloon at the cup end with tightly wound string. Pull it back into the cup, then seal the cup with plastic wrap and a rubber band.

3. Tape a bent paper clip handle to the plastic wrap. Pull it in and out to make the cup "breathe!"

   a. This apparatus models your own respiratory system. Draw a diagram labeling those parts that represent your *lungs, diaphragm* and *trachea*.

   b. Use this model to explain why air enters your lungs as you inhale; why air exits your lungs as you exhale.

   c. Take apart your model and save the parts.

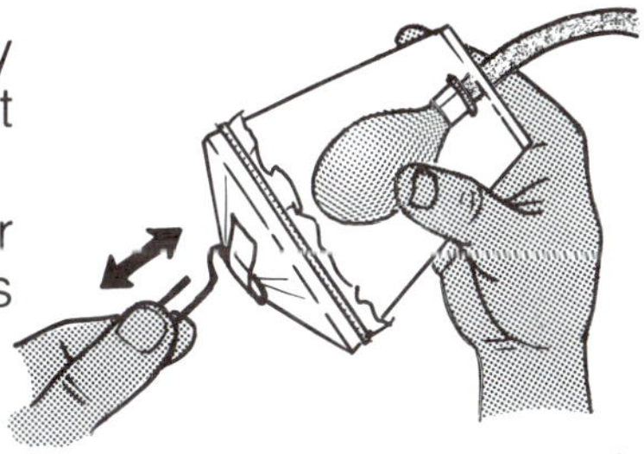

© 1992 by TOPS Learning Systems

BUBBLES UP   Pressure (   )

1. Cover the bottom of a tub with about 2 cm of water, up to the first joint of your little finger.

2. Fill a jar brimful with water, cover with a canning lid, then invert in the water.

3. Slide the lid away, then raise the jar onto 3 washers. Be sure to keep its rim under water at all times.

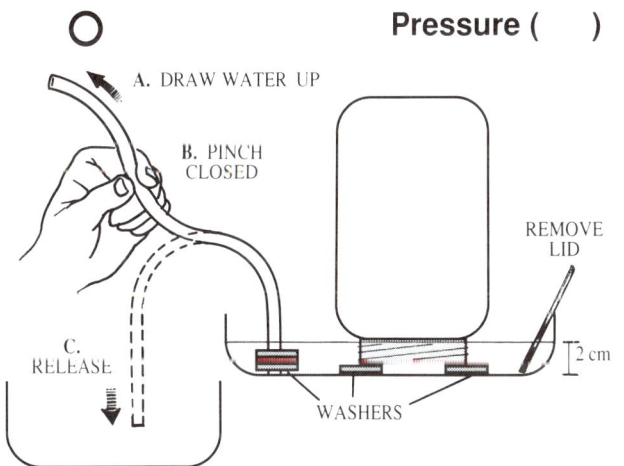

4. Weigh down the end of a tube with washers. Suck water up through this tube, but pinch its end closed before the water reaches your mouth.

5. Release the water into a *lower* container or sink.

   a. What happens to the water? Fully describe what you see.

   b. What makes the water *siphon* (flow to a lower level)?

   c. The fall of water inside the jar is jerky rather than smooth. Explain why.

© 1992 by TOPS Learning Systems

cards 9-10

A CLOSED SYSTEM ◯ Pressure ( )

1. Punch a nail hole through the center of a canning lid resting on a jar.

2. Flip the lid to the bottom side. Center a washer over the hole, and tape the edges firmly.

BOTTOM VIEW:
TAPE
NAIL HOLE

3. Firmly hold the washer against the lid. Use a round tapered tool to first drill down from the top, then up from the bottom, enlarging the nail hole to washer-hole size.

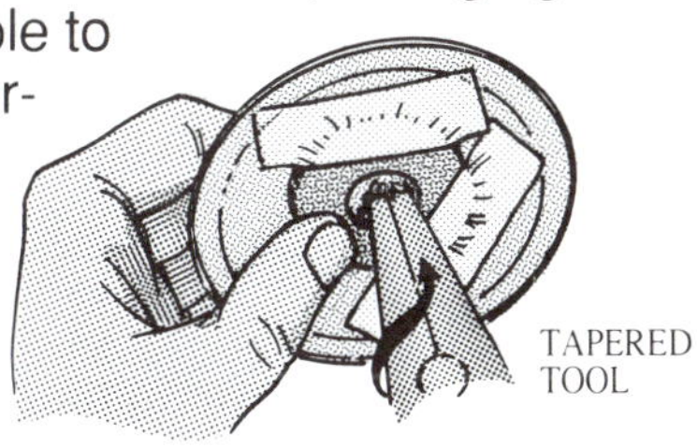

TAPERED TOOL

4. Smooth back all metal fragments to secure the washer, then remove the tape.

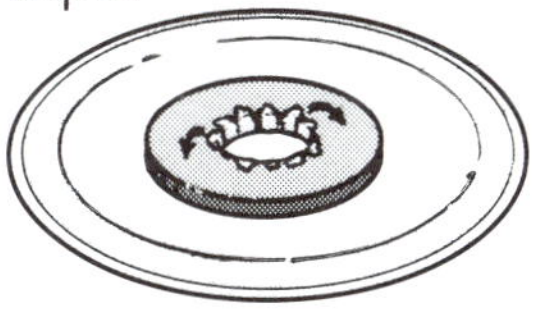

5. Half fill an eyedropper with water and place it in the jar. Seal the lid on with a canning ring, and fit a tube into the hole.

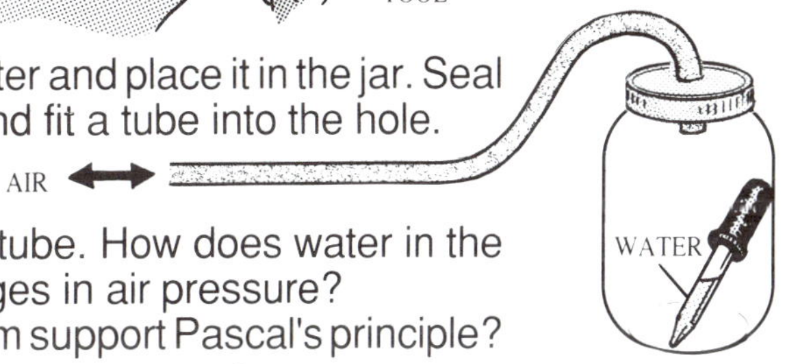

AIR ⇄
WATER

a. Force air in and out of the tube. How does water in the eyedropper respond to changes in air pressure?
b. How does this closed system support Pascal's principle?

© 1992 by TOPS Learning Systems

11

SUBMARINE ◯ Pressure ( )

1. Fill an eyedropper with enough water so it *barely* floats in a quart jar.

2. Using a canning lid (without holes) and a ring, seal this dropper in a quart jar *brimful* of water.

3. Press down on the lid to make your dropper dive. If it doesn't sink, draw a little more water into the dropper and try again.

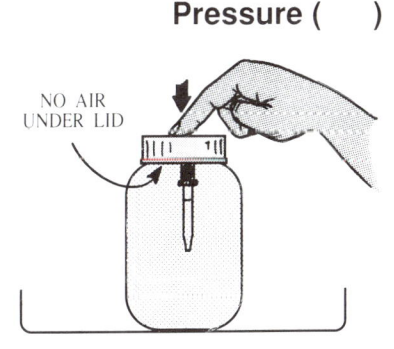

NO AIR UNDER LID

4. The eyedropper sinks and floats as water moves in and out of it. Use Pascal's principle to explain why this happens.

5. Cut the head off a wooden match, leaving no excess wood. Float it in a test tube brimful of water, then make it sink and float by pressing with your thumb.

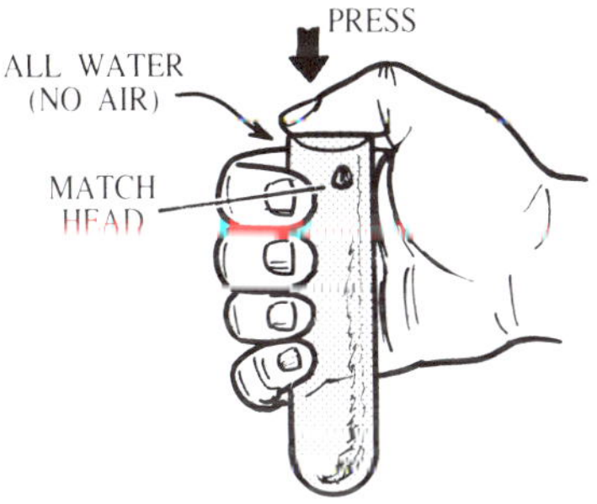

PRESS
ALL WATER (NO AIR)
MATCH HEAD

a. What physical changes in the match head might cause it to rise and fall?
b. Use arrows to diagram how pressure from your thumb is distributed through the water.

© 1992 by TOPS Learning Systems

12

cards 11-12

BUILD A MANOMETER ○ Pressure (   )

1. Cut out the Pressure Scale and tape it to the side panel of a cereal box, with the zero mark half-way to the top.

2. Fix 80 cm of tubing to this scale with 2 rubber bands stretched firmly, but not too tightly. Keep excess tubing to the left, and a broad, gentle curve at the bottom.

3. Fill the box 1/3 full with gravel, sand or dirt for stability. Seal the top shut with tape.

4. Fill the bottom of the U-bend with water tinted by food coloring. Add just enough to reach the zero mark.

5. *Gently* blow or suck on the tube, taking care that no liquid leaves the U. How do water levels change when your mouth is…
   a. *pressurized* (greater than atmospheric pressure)?
   b. *evacuated* (less than atmospheric pressure)?

6. Does your *manometer* (pressure gauge) measure the *total* pressure in your mouth or a *difference* in pressure? Explain.

© 1992 by TOPS Learning Systems   13

CENTIMETERS OF WATER ○ Pressure (   )

1. Punch 2 holes through a canning lid with a nail. Use washers to get the correct spacing.

2. Drill out each hole with a washer underneath, as you did in activity 11.

3. Connect your manometer plus a second tube to a jar. Seal all joints airtight with grease.

4. Evacuate the jar 4 cm *from zero*. Hold this pressure with a clothespin throughout this step.
   a. Is your system airtight? How do you know? If not, fix it.
   b. What is the *difference* in air pressure, measured in cm of water, inside and outside the jar?
   c. If you could pump every last molecule of air out of your jar to create a *perfect vacuum,* the water levels (in a manometer very much taller than this one) would separate 1034 cm! How high does 1034 cm reach?
   d. If the atmosphere supports 1034 cm of water, what is the *total* pressure now in your jar?

5. Take off the clothespin, then place the end of the tube into a jar of water.
   a. How does water pressure change with depth?
   b. Do you think this relationship holds for other fluids, like air? Explain.

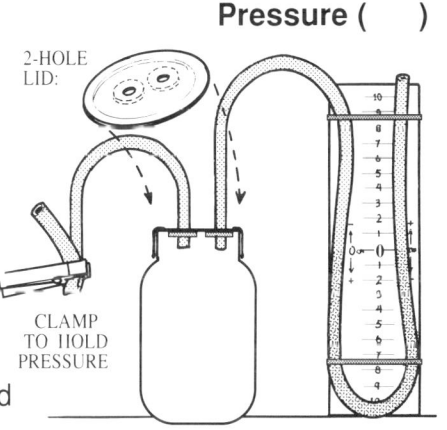

© 1992 by TOPS Learning Systems   14

cards 13-14

U TUBE / STRAIGHT TUBE   Pressure (   )

1. Construct a 3-hole lid with washers, similar to your 1-hole and 2-hole lids.

2. Attach 2 tubes plus your manometer with air-tight seals. Feed one of the tubes through the top rubber band of your manometer, then down into a small jar of tinted water.

3. Gently evacuate the large jar. Notice that it is now connected to *two* different manometers.
   a. How is the new manometer different?
   b. Do they both indicate the same pressure?
   c. Where is the water in each manometer exposed to Earth's atmosphere?

4. Replace the small jar of colored water with a pie tin half full of clear water. Connect your 1-hole cup to the tube, and seal airtight.
   a. Does each gauge still register the same pressure?
   b. Should pressure be measured by the *volume* of water it supports, or its *height*? Explain.

© 1992 by TOPS Learning Systems

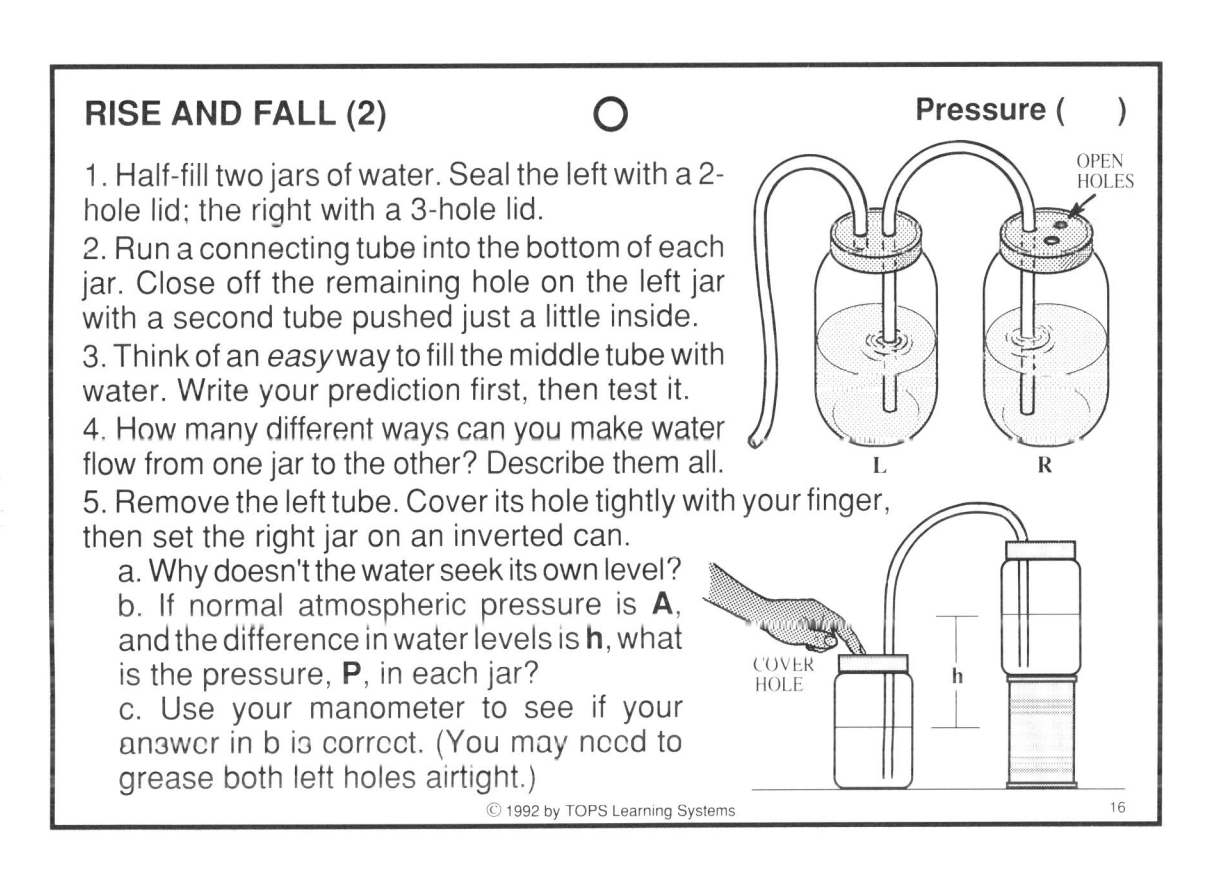

RISE AND FALL (2)   Pressure (   )

1. Half-fill two jars of water. Seal the left with a 2-hole lid; the right with a 3-hole lid.

2. Run a connecting tube into the bottom of each jar. Close off the remaining hole on the left jar with a second tube pushed just a little inside.

3. Think of an *easy* way to fill the middle tube with water. Write your prediction first, then test it.

4. How many different ways can you make water flow from one jar to the other? Describe them all.

5. Remove the left tube. Cover its hole tightly with your finger, then set the right jar on an inverted can.
   a. Why doesn't the water seek its own level?
   b. If normal atmospheric pressure is **A**, and the difference in water levels is **h**, what is the pressure, **P**, in each jar?
   c. Use your manometer to see if your answer in b is correct. (You may need to grease both left holes airtight.)

© 1992 by TOPS Learning Systems

cards 15-16

RISE AND FALL (3)   Pressure ( )

1. Fill a jar half full of water and seal it with your two-hole lid. Insert 2 tubes into the holes as shown. Attach your 1-hole plastic cup to the tube that extends to the bottom of the jar.

   a. Raise the pressure in the jar below, until you fill the cup above. Does it matter how high you hold the cup? Explain.

   b. What is the maximum pressure, in cm of water, that the higher cup exerts on the lower jar?

   c. Can you control the flow of water from jar to cup without changing the air pressure? Explain.

2. Push the other tube below the water so *both* touch the bottom of the jar. Grease both lid holes to assure an airtight seal.

   a. Raise the pressure in the lower jar once more. What happens differently? Cite 3 differences, explaining each one.

   b. Use this apparatus to show that *height,* not *volume,* is the appropriate variable to measure pressure.

© 1992 by TOPS Learning Systems   17

INFLOW / OUTFLOW   Pressure ( )

1. Nearly fill a jar with water, and raise it on a can. Connect it to a nearly empty jar with a funnel, tubes and clothespin as shown. (Note: The water tube and funnel both extend to the bottom of a jar. Clip them together with a clothespin that *partially* constricts the tube's opening.)

2. Wipe the funnel joint and extra hole free of moisture and grease, then seal them airtight with clay. Seal all tube joints with grease.

3. Pour a little water into the funnel until it begins to pour out of the water tube.

   a. Why does this happen?
   b. Why does it continue?
   c. What would happen if the funnel did not extend under the water?
   d. Why does the water finally stop flowing?

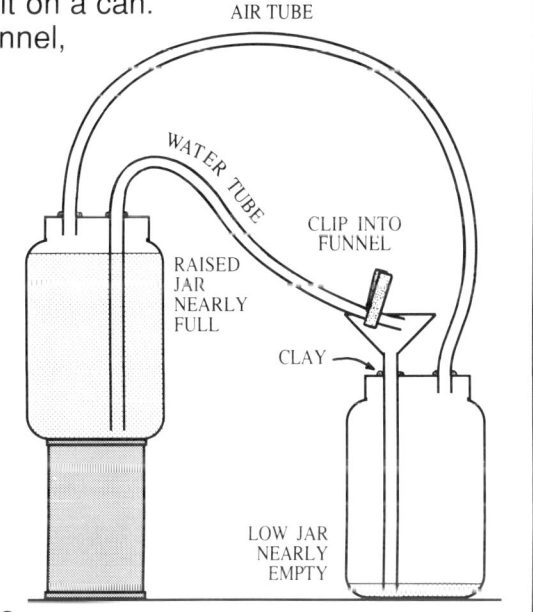

© 1992 by TOPS Learning Systems   18

cards 17-18

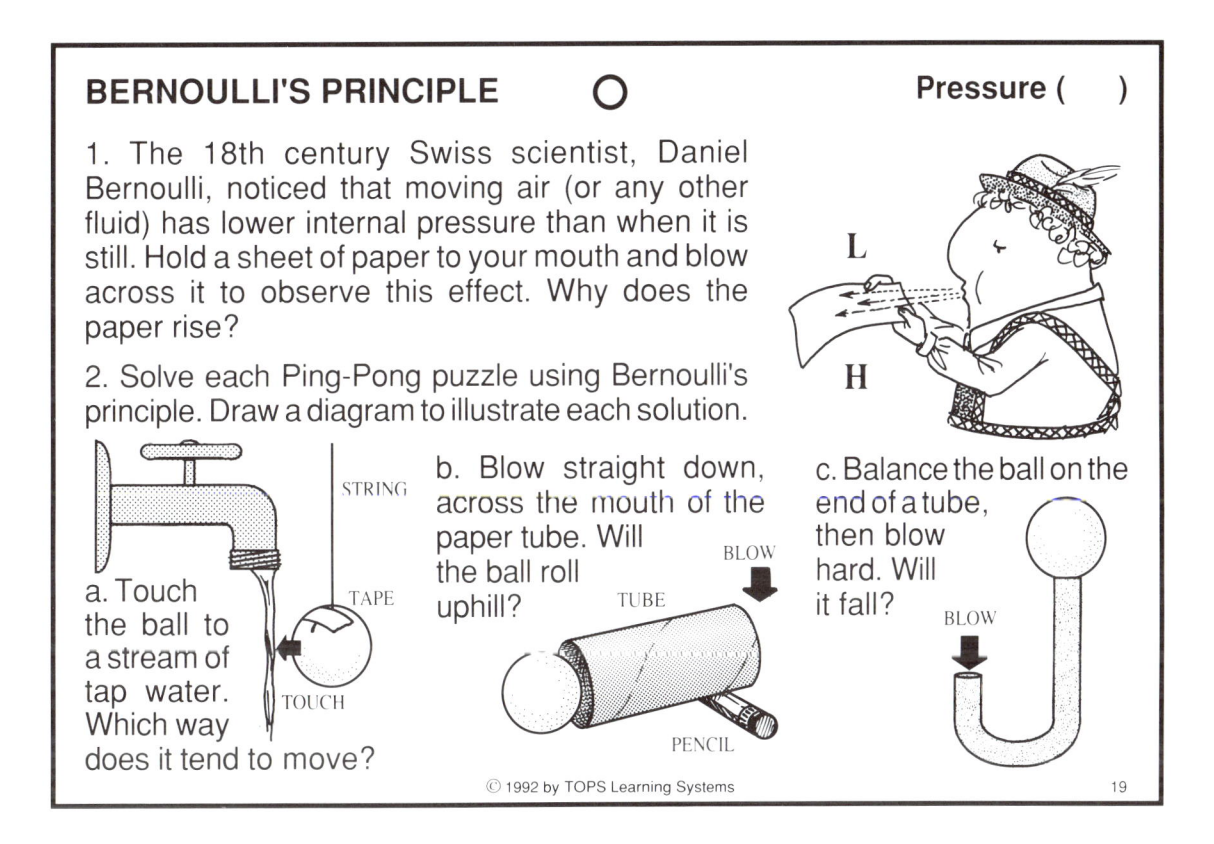

BERNOULLI'S PRINCIPLE ○   Pressure (   )

1. The 18th century Swiss scientist, Daniel Bernoulli, noticed that moving air (or any other fluid) has lower internal pressure than when it is still. Hold a sheet of paper to your mouth and blow across it to observe this effect. Why does the paper rise?

2. Solve each Ping-Pong puzzle using Bernoulli's principle. Draw a diagram to illustrate each solution.

a. Touch the ball to a stream of tap water. Which way does it tend to move?

b. Blow straight down, across the mouth of the paper tube. Will the ball roll uphill?

c. Balance the ball on the end of a tube, then blow hard. Will it fall?

© 1992 by TOPS Learning Systems

19

ATOMIZERS ○   Pressure (   )

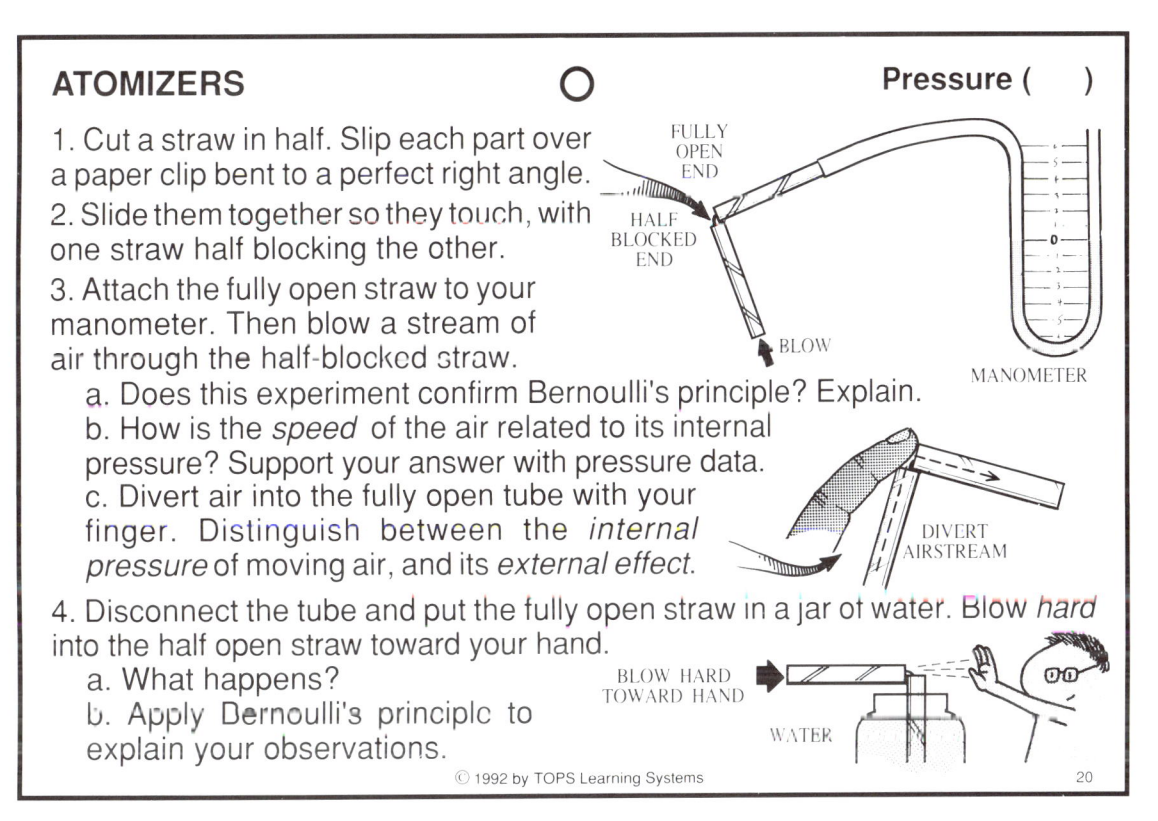

1. Cut a straw in half. Slip each part over a paper clip bent to a perfect right angle.
2. Slide them together so they touch, with one straw half blocking the other.
3. Attach the fully open straw to your manometer. Then blow a stream of air through the half-blocked straw.
    a. Does this experiment confirm Bernoulli's principle? Explain.
    b. How is the *speed* of the air related to its internal pressure? Support your answer with pressure data.
    c. Divert air into the fully open tube with your finger. Distinguish between the *internal pressure* of moving air, and its *external effect*.
4. Disconnect the tube and put the fully open straw in a jar of water. Blow *hard* into the half open straw toward your hand.
    a. What happens?
    b. Apply Bernoulli's principle to explain your observations.

© 1992 by TOPS Learning Systems

20

cards 19-20

AIRFOIL ○ Pressure ( )

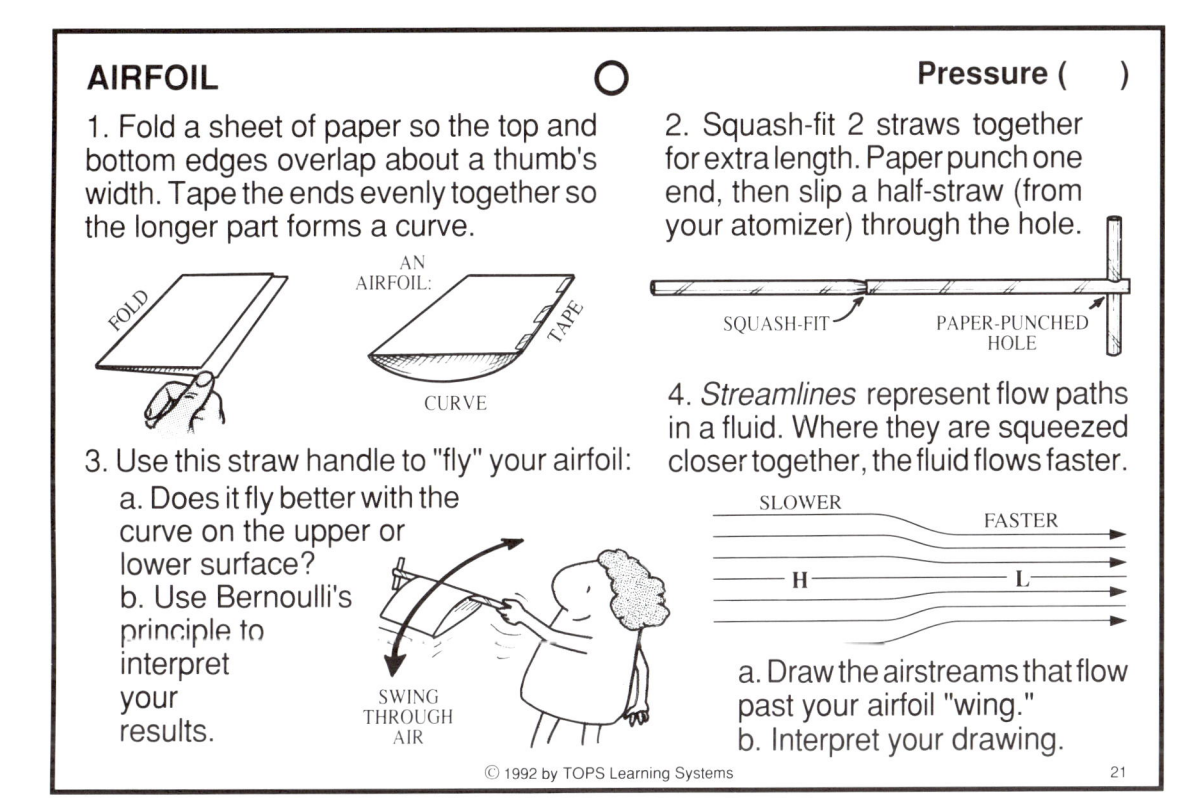

1. Fold a sheet of paper so the top and bottom edges overlap about a thumb's width. Tape the ends evenly together so the longer part forms a curve.

2. Squash-fit 2 straws together for extra length. Paper punch one end, then slip a half-straw (from your atomizer) through the hole.

SQUASH-FIT   PAPER-PUNCHED HOLE

4. *Streamlines* represent flow paths in a fluid. Where they are squeezed closer together, the fluid flows faster.

SLOWER   FASTER
H   L

3. Use this straw handle to "fly" your airfoil:
   a. Does it fly better with the curve on the upper or lower surface?
   b. Use Bernoulli's principle to interpret your results.

SWING THROUGH AIR

   a. Draw the airstreams that flow past your airfoil "wing."
   b. Interpret your drawing.

© 1992 by TOPS Learning Systems   21

SPIN AND CURVE ○ Pressure ( )

1. Cut a cardboard tube in half along its length. Lightly tape one of the halves to a book.

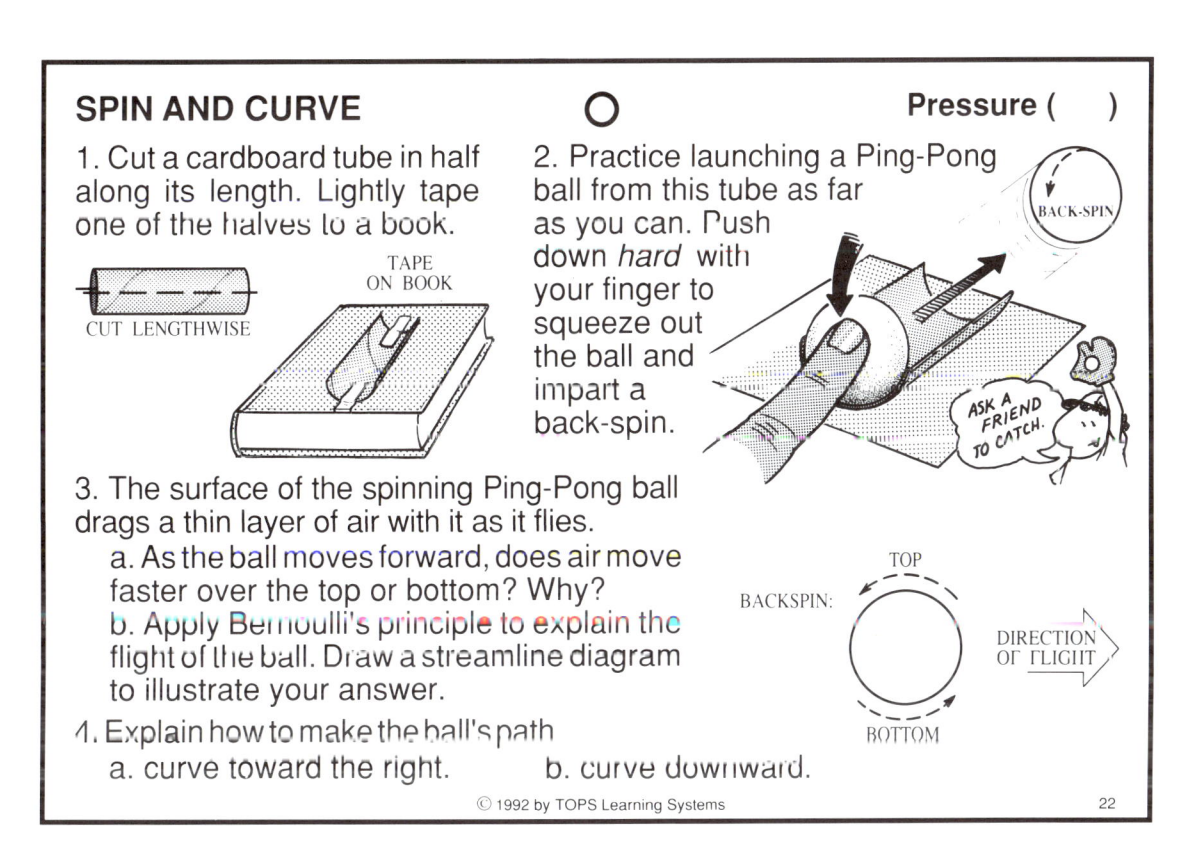

CUT LENGTHWISE   TAPE ON BOOK

2. Practice launching a Ping-Pong ball from this tube as far as you can. Push down *hard* with your finger to squeeze out the ball and impart a back-spin.

BACK-SPIN

ASK A FRIEND TO CATCH.

3. The surface of the spinning Ping-Pong ball drags a thin layer of air with it as it flies.
   a. As the ball moves forward, does air move faster over the top or bottom? Why?
   b. Apply Bernoulli's principle to explain the flight of the ball. Draw a streamline diagram to illustrate your answer.

BACKSPIN:
TOP
BOTTOM
DIRECTION OF FLIGHT

4. Explain how to make the ball's path
   a. curve toward the right.   b. curve downward.

© 1992 by TOPS Learning Systems   22

cards 21-22

STEAM TO STREAM   Pressure (   )

1. Add about 2 cm of water to a small test tube, and hold its *center* with a clothespin or test tube clamp. Position a jar of water nearby that is nearly full of water.

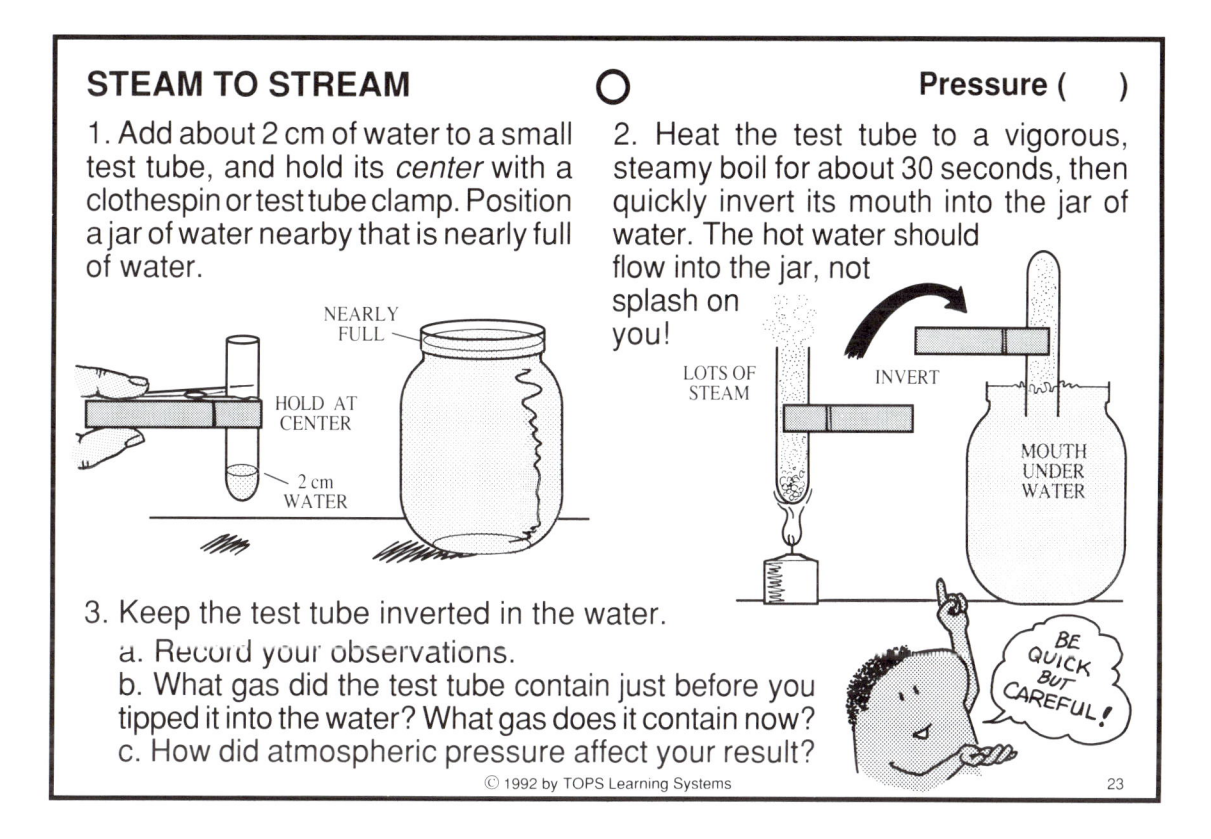

2. Heat the test tube to a vigorous, steamy boil for about 30 seconds, then quickly invert its mouth into the jar of water. The hot water should flow into the jar, not splash on you!

3. Keep the test tube inverted in the water.
   a. Record your observations.
   b. What gas did the test tube contain just before you tipped it into the water? What gas does it contain now?
   c. How did atmospheric pressure affect your result?

© 1992 by TOPS Learning Systems

A PERFECT VACUUM?   Pressure (   )

1. Roll clay into an egg-shaped cap, so it rests on the mouth of a test tube like this:

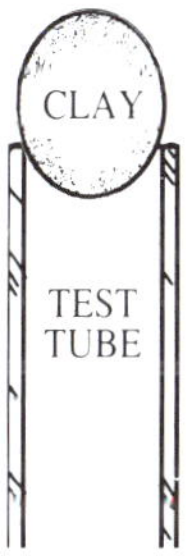

2. Heat about 2 cm of water in your *open* test tube to a steamy boil for about 30 seconds, holding it at the top. Remove it from the flame while pressing in the clay cap *at the same time*, taking care not to burn your fingers on the steam.

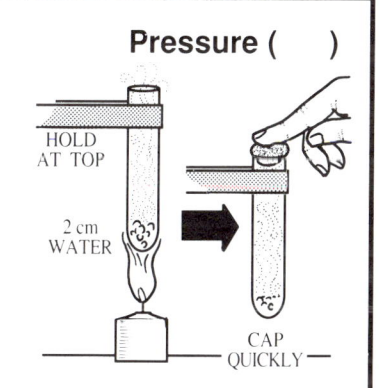

3. Allow your sealed test tube to cool to room temperature.
   a. Does atmospheric pressure now affect your test tube in any visible way?
   b. A *perfect vacuum* is empty space that contains no matter at all. Do you think your test tube now contains a perfect vacuum? Explain.

4. Predict what will happen if you break the clay seal under water. Give reasons for your answer.
   a. Test your prediction.
   b. Does your result indicate that you achieved a *perfect* vacuum? Explain.

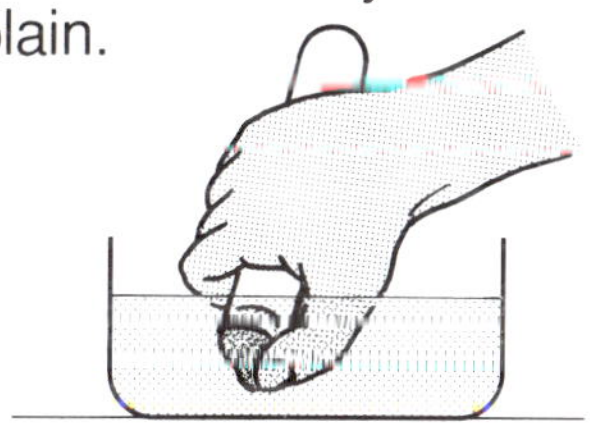

© 1992 by TOPS Learning Systems

A VERY TALL TEST TUBE   Pressure (   )

1. Press a paper cap over the mouth of a test tube of water, and invert it over a tub. The atmosphere holds this water in with a pressure of roughly 10 N/cm². Does water press this hard from the inside? Explain.

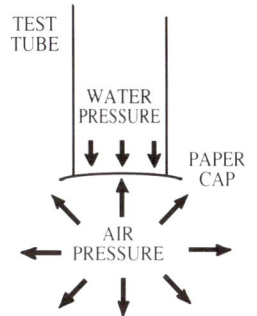

2. Empty and dry your tube. Trim a wedge of paper to fit the inside diameter. Use this to estimate its cross-sectional area in cm².

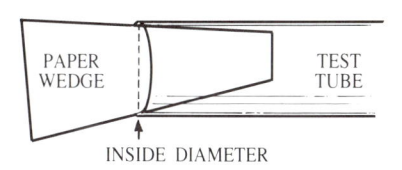

3. You will now calculate the maximum height a test tube full of water can reach, and still have all its water supported by atmospheric pressure.
   a. If 1 ml of water weighs about .01 Newton, use a graduated cylinder to estimate the total weight of water in your full tube.
   b. Calculate the water's pressure at the mouth of your inverted tube. How many times stronger is the atmospheric pressure that holds it up?
   c. Measure the height of your test tube in centimeters. How much higher could this tube of water reach before atmospheric pressure is overcome and the water falls out?

© 1992 by TOPS Learning Systems

25

MEASURE THE PRESSURE   Pressure (   )

1. The right amount of water in a plastic milk jug, when pulling straight down on the plunger of a sealed plastic syringe, will *slowly* open a vacuum in its chamber.
   a. Identify two kinds of forces overcome by this water jug.
   b. Experiment to find the volume of water needed to overcome these combined forces.

2. Find the volume of water needed to overcome friction *alone;* atmospheric pressure *alone*. Show your work.

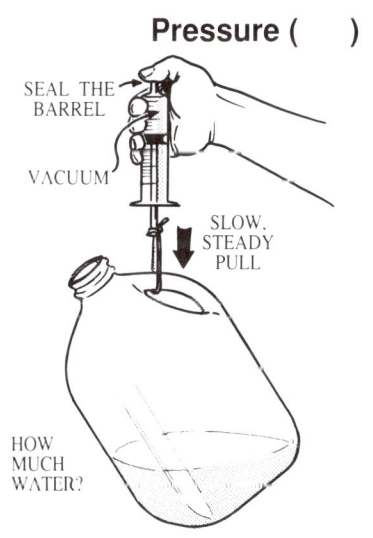

3. Calculate atmospheric pressure:
   a. Trim a wedge of paper to measure the inside diameter of your syringe. Use this to estimate its cross-sectional area in cm².
   b. Knowing that water weighs about .01 N/ml, find the total force distributed over this much area.
   c. Divide to find the pressure. How close did you come to the accepted rough value of 10 N/cm²?

© 1992 by TOPS Learning Systems

26

cards 25-26

VACUUM PUMP ◯ Pressure ( )

1. Take the bulb off an eyedropper. Fit a piece of tubing, as long as the barrel, over the glass rim.

TUBING
GLASS BARREL

2. Drop a BB into its nose. Slip the nose of a second eyedropper into the tube, then draw water up by squeezing the bulb.
   a. What can you discover?
   b. Would this happen without the BB? Without atmospheric pressure? Explain.

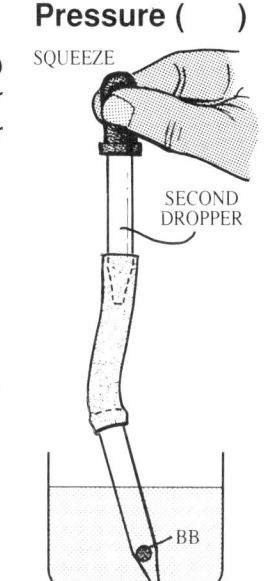

SQUEEZE
SECOND DROPPER
BB

3. Replace the bulb on your second dropper with a longer tube. Use this to build a vacuum pump that lifts water from a lower jar to a higher jar resting on a can.
   a. Diagram your solution.
   b. Explain how your vacuum pump works.
   c. What is the maximum height that a vacuum pump (even a high-tech one) can lift water? Why?
   d. Can you think of a way to pump water higher than this limitation?
   e. Take your pump apart. Put the bulbs back on the dropper barrels.

© 1992 by TOPS Learning Systems   27

BATTERY PRESSURE ◯ Pressure ( )

1. Calculate the pressure (in N/cm^2) applied to the flat end of a size-D dry cell by a closed, empty quart jar resting above it.

Recall that $1\ g \cong .01\ N$.

JAR CLOSED
HOW MUCH PRESSURE?
STEADY THE JAR.
FLAT END

2. Your task is to now increase this pressure to 1/10 atmospheric pressure, about $1\ N/cm^2$.
   a. How many Newtons of weight must press down on the end of the battery to achieve this pressure?
   b. Recall that 1 ml water $\cong$ 1 g. How much water must you add to the jar to achieve this pressure?
   c. Fill a jar with this much water and seal it tightly.
   d. Label the jar with an appropriate title and tape the battery to the top.

© 1992 by TOPS Learning Systems   28

MAXIMUM LUNG PRESSURE? ○ Pressure ( )

1. Gather the mouth of a sandwich bag around the end of a tube. Seal with at least 10 turns of string covered with tape.
2. Cut scratch paper in half the short way. Roll it evenly around a size-D battery and secure with tape.
3. Punch a hole, just above the dry cell, with a nail. Thread your tube through this hole so the bag fits inside.
4. Adjust the bag so it puffs out the top only about 2 cm when you blow into the tube.
   a. Use this small "air bag" and your labeled jar with battery from the previous activity to estimate your maximum lung pressure.
   b. Why is it important to start with the bag *entirely* inside the tube?

© 1992 by TOPS Learning Systems

BIG LIFT ○ Pressure ( )

1. Take apart your air bag assembly from the last activity. Attach a larger produce bag to the end of the tube with at least 10 turns of string, as before.

2. Flatten the bag, smoothing it out to its maximum 2-dimensional size. Estimate its top (or bottom) surface area with two centimeter grids taped together. Recall how you did this in activity 2.

3. Recall your maximum lung pressure determined in the previous activity.
   a. Use this value to estimate the maximum weight, in Newtons, that you can lift with this bag.
   b. Convert your answer to pounds. (1 N = .22 lbs)
   c. The maximum force you can lift with this bag decreases as you continue to blow air into it. Explain why.

4. Test your prediction using body weight. Explain what you did.

© 1992 by TOPS Learning Systems

Area Estimator: Square Inches (in²)

Area Estimator: Square Centimeters (cm²)

Pressure Scale (activity 13)

Centimeter Ruler (activity 1)

Copyright © 1992 by TOPS Learning Systems.

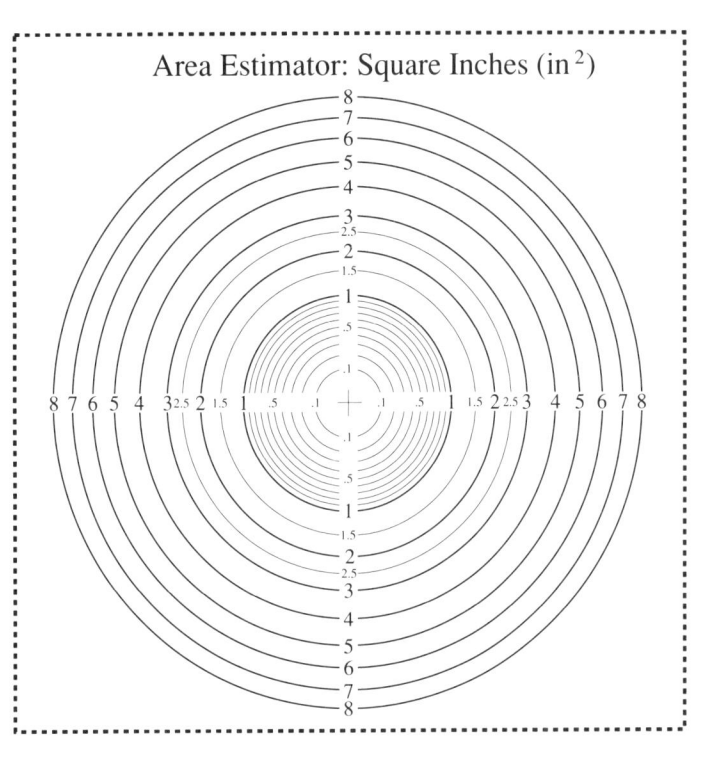

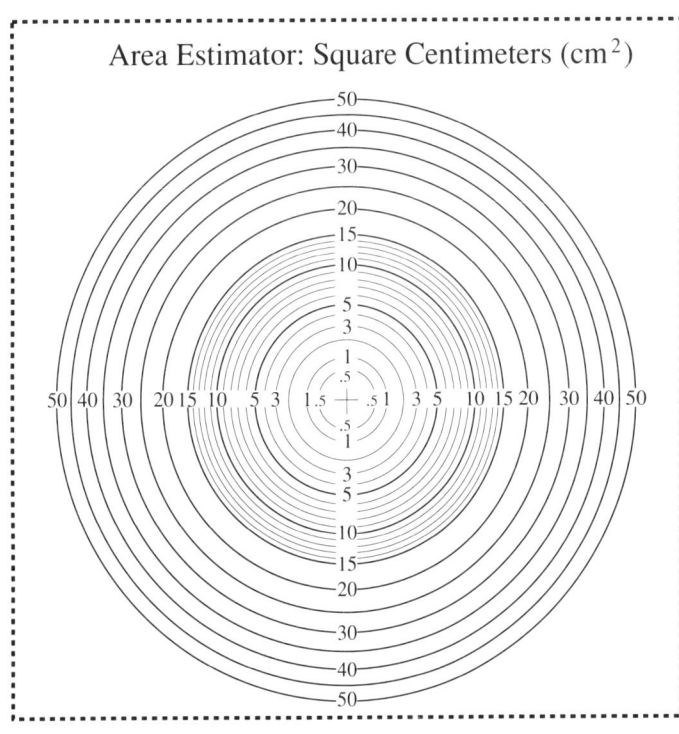

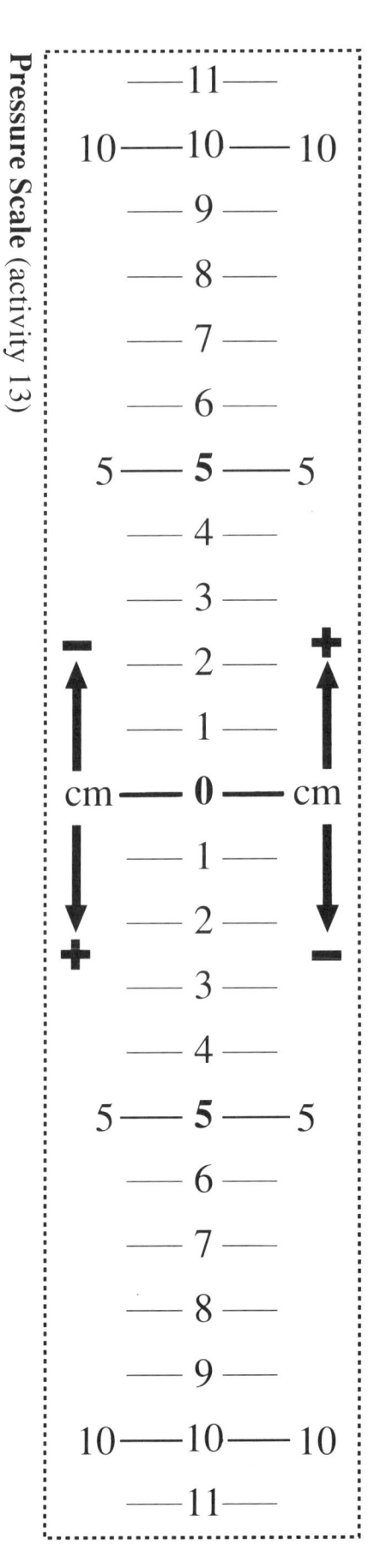

THREE VARIABLES   Pressure ( )

1. Connect your manometer to a jar with a 1-hole lid. Seal it airtight with grease.

2. Warm the jar with your hands. Cool it with a paper towel dampened with rubbing alcohol.

a. Complete this table.

TEMP	PRESSURE
INCREASE	
DECREASE	

b. Consider these equations:

$$P = kT, \quad P = k/T$$

← (k is any constant number) →

Which one best summarizes your observations? Explain.

3. Squeeze and relax the tube between the jar and manometer. This compresses and expands the volume of air inside the closed system.

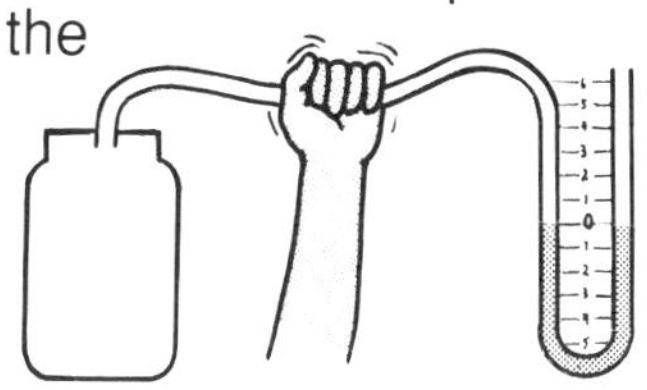

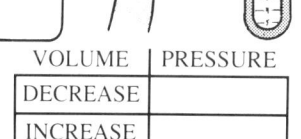

a. Complete this table.

VOLUME	PRESSURE
DECREASE	
INCREASE	

b. Consider these equations:

$$P = kV, \quad P = k/V$$

Which one best summarizes your observations? Explain.

4. Consider these equations: $PT = kV$, $PV = kT$, $VT = kP$. Which one best summarizes all observations in this activity? Explain your reasoning.

© 1992 by TOPS Learning Systems   31

ANEROID BAROMETER   Pressure ( )

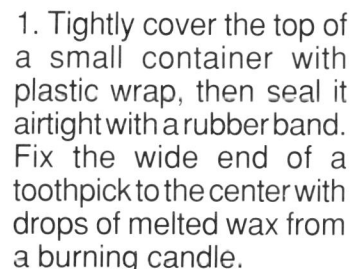

1. Tightly cover the top of a small container with plastic wrap, then seal it airtight with a rubber band. Fix the wide end of a toothpick to the center with drops of melted wax from a burning candle.

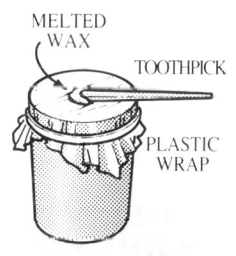

2. After the wax hardens, carefully place the entire assembly in the bottom of a jar. Seal with your 1-hole lid and insert a rubber tube.

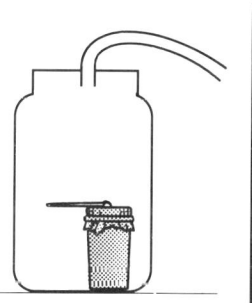

3. A *barometer* measures changes in atmospheric pressure. An *aneroid* barometer does this without liquid.
   a. How do the plastic wrap and toothpick respond as you change the air pressure inside the jar?
   b. Have you made an aneroid barometer? Explain.

4. This device is probably not sensitive enough to measure the high pressure of a sunny day, or the low pressure of a rainy day.
   a. Design and build a larger, more sensitive instrument. Use it to forecast changes in the weather.
   b. What *other* variable must be kept constant to accurately track changes in atmospheric pressure? Explain.

© 1992 by TOPS Learning Systems   32

CENTIMETER GRID